THE COMING INTERNET DEPRESSION

THE COMING INTERNET DEPRESSION

Why the High-Tech Boom Will Go Bust,
Why the Crash Will Be Worse Than You
Think, and How to Prosper Afterwards

MICHAEL J. MANDEL

BASIC
BOOKS

A Member of the Perseus Books Group

A CIP catalog record for this book is available from the Library of
Congress.

ISBN: 0-465-04358-5

Designed by Nighthawk Design

FIRST EDITION

00 01 02 03 / 10 9 8 7 6 5 4 3 2 1

To Elliot and Laura,
my loving children

Contents

Preface

UNLIKE MOST economists and economic journalists, I take seriously the idea that the U.S. has a "New Economy" that is not just a juiced-up version of the old industrial economy. I believe in the power of the Internet and the information revolution to transform our lives. Since the industrial revolution started, every century has had faster growth than the previous one, and our own will be no different. Our children will live better than we do, and despite doubts about the future of Social Security, the baby boomers will be able to retire successfully and prosper. And with any luck, the New Economy will spread to the rest of the world as well.

But as I wrote in *Business Week* in 1998, "the New Economy has never been about sunny skies forever."[1] There is a good chance that the New Economy boom will be followed by a New Economy bust. If policymakers do not take the right measures, the bust could turn into an Internet Depression—an extended period of stagnation during which much of the economic gains of recent years will be lost. It's important to face up to this dark side; hence this book.

One of my goals is to counteract the complacency of two groups who would be willing to stand by and do nothing as the Internet Depression unfolds. One group is made up of the skeptical economists who are still convinced that the U.S. economy's performance in the 1990s was simply a one-time technology "shock." These hard-core doubters would welcome a downturn as a return to normalcy. The other group includes the true believers in the power of the information revolution to defeat the business cycle, who have faith that the new technology means growth everlasting. Each side is, in its own way, dangerously wrong.

Another objective is to help the ordinary investor, business executive, and worker understand what is happening to the economy as it slides downward. Decisions made during the slump—buy or sell, invest or hunker down, take career risks or play it safe, keep spending or pay off debts—will go a long way toward determining who prospers in the years to come.

Finally, I'd like to offer some hope for the future. If and when the Internet Depression does hit with full force, it will feel like the New Economy was just a mirage. But the New Economy is very real, and when the slump is over—one year, five years, or ten years later—the good times will resume. After all, the U.S. economy eventually rebounded from the Depression, and the people who grew up in the tough years of the 1930s ended up raising their families in the 1950s and 1960s, the Golden Era of American capitalism. With any luck, and good policy, the same thing will happen again.

Acknowledgments

In many ways this book is an outgrowth of the work I've done at *Business Week* for the past eleven years. I'd like to thank Steve Shepard, editor-in-chief of *Business Week,* for all his support over the years. My thanks, too, to Chris Farrell, Seymour Zucker, Bill Wolman, Bruce Nussbaum, William Frucht of Basic Books, and Sarah Chalfant of the Wylie Agency. And of course my infinite appreciation goes to Judy Scherer, without whom the book could never have been written.

THE COMING INTERNET DEPRESSION

CHAPTER ONE

Peril and Promise

*The business cycle—a creation of the Industrial Age—may
well become an anachronism.*

—*Wall Street Journal,* December 31, 1999[1]

EVERY ECONOMIC ERA is afflicted by its own unique curse.
Agricultural economies were tied to the rhythms of the harvests.
Villages would prosper when crops were good, and suffer when
drought or pests withered the fields. A long enough drought
could devastate a region or even a civilization. "Up until the business cycle of 1857, or perhaps 1866, the harvest was the measure
of business conditions," wrote the economic historian Charles
Kindleberger. "A bumper crop lowered the price of bread. . . .
Crop failure, on the other hand, led to depression."[2]

Trading economies, like that of England in the 1600s, were
considerably less affected by a failed harvest in a single location,
since they could import food if necessary. But the growing
importance of overseas trade introduced new sources of unpredictable fluctuations. The opening up of new trading opportunities could create a burst of new wealth and prosperity. Alter-
natively, a flood of gold or silver from overseas—as when Spain
conquered Mexico—could ignite an inflationary boom. The
free flow of goods between nations was regularly impeded by

war, religious disputes, and deliberate currency manipulations by governments. The result, according to one historian, was that "variations in prosperity were random and discontinuous."[3]

The gradual shift to an industrial economy seemingly made growth more controllable and predictable. No longer was prosperity tied to the harvest or the vagaries of colonial exploitation. The new source of wealth was systematic investment in capital goods—machinery, factories, railroads, electrical, and telephone systems—which could be used to multiply human productivity. At the same time, the rise of the modern stock and bond markets in the second half of the 1800s provided financing for large capital projects on a scale never before dreamed of. The dawn of mass production permitted industrial economies to achieve unprecedented growth rates and living standards.

It soon became clear, however, that industrial economies were prone to new types of economic fluctuations. Worse, these shocks were broader, more pervasive, and in many ways more violent than any country had experienced before. Starting in the middle of the 19th century, national and global capital markets opened up the door, for the first time, to national and global economic crises—the boom-and-bust cycles in business investment and labor markets that we now recognize as the familiar business cycle.

In the early 20th century, housing and consumer durables such as autos joined the business cycle as well. Easy credit would fuel overinvestment and overproduction, which would be followed by a sharp recession and a daunting rise in unemployment. The stock market and banking systems necessary for funding long-term capital investments could go badly awry, paralyzing an economy dependent on credit. The result was a series of national and international economic downturns, including deep ones in 1873, 1893, 1907, 1920, and of course 1929.[4] The last event, especially, raised fears that modern industrial economies were simply too unstable to be trusted.

But over time, and after intense arguments, economists and policymakers figured out ways to manage the instability of market economies—a triumph of which economists were justifiably proud. As economist Paul Krugman wrote, "In effect, capitalism and its economists made a deal with the public; it will be okay to have free markets from now on, because we know enough to prevent any more Great Depressions."[5]

Measures such as deposit insurance and unemployment insurance were put in place to protect the industrial economy from its own worst excesses. Washington policymakers at the Federal Reserve Board, the White House, and Congress learned how to use monetary and fiscal policy to manage the ups and downs of the business cycle, cutting interest rates and taxes and boosting government spending to jump-start growth when recession loomed. The central bankers at the Fed, despite their innate caution, learned to embrace the obligations of "lender of last resort." That meant they had a responsibility, no matter what, to move quickly to pump money into the financial system whenever it looked like it might unravel.

True, the rule book for managing the business cycle did have to be rewritten several times. Deficits or surpluses in the federal budget came to be seen as far less important for regulating the business cycle than monetary policy. In the aftermath of the inflationary surge of the 1970s, policymakers became much more concerned with making sure the economy didn't overheat. By the beginning of the 1990s, economists were fairly confident that they understood how to avoid (or at least soften) the business cycle's highs and lows.

Enter the New Economy, also known as the Information Economy, the Internet Economy, or the 21st Century Economy. Built around the high-tech revolution and globalization, the New Economy seemed partially immune from the ills that plagued the old industrial economy, just as the industrial economy was partially immune from the vagaries of the harvest. A computerized and networked supply chain allowed the real-time monitoring of inventories, so production never got too far ahead of sales. The combination of soaring productivity and intense competition, at home and abroad, kept inflation in check despite low unemployment rates. That meant that instead of acting aggressively to slow the economy, the Federal Reserve Board could afford to let growth roll.

In February 2000, the expansion that started in March 1991 became the longest period of uninterrupted growth in U.S. history. This milestone provoked a burst of enthusiasm from journalists, economists, business executives, and investors, both in the U.S. and elsewhere—even many who had been skeptical about the New Economy. More and more people were willing to consider the notion that the expansion never needed to end.

It would be wonderful if it turns out we have reached the promised land. Given the misery that recessions and depressions have caused over the years, any moderation of these fluctuations would be a major benefit of the New Economy. What's more, the elimination of the business cycle, if it turns out to be real, would reduce the risk of investing in equities and justify the lofty valuation of the stock market.

NEW ECONOMY, NEW PROBLEMS

But each economic era is afflicted by its own unique curse. The New Economy is not simply a more cosmopolitan version of the old industrial economy, a faster model with better suspension and steering. It is something very different.

One of the great strengths of the New Economy—and its great flaw as well—is the blossoming of a systematic market mechanism devoted to finding and funding technological and business innovation on a large scale. This mechanism includes venture capital funds, which funnel money from pension funds and other large investors into high-risk, high-return new businesses; stock exchanges that easily allow new firms to go public; a large pool of sophisticated risk-taking capital; and a cohort of skilled workers who are willing to take chances on working for new firms, in exchange for the prospect of stock options and future wealth.

The result: As new technologies arise, the availability of risk capital can greatly accelerate their application and adoption. Here, for the first time, are the beginnings of a marketplace in which entrepreneurs with bright ideas can actually get enough money to challenge existing companies. Netscape could find enough money to throw a big fright into Microsoft, the dominant software firm of its day. Amazon.com could find money to scare the preeminent bookstore chain, Barnes and Noble, into radically changing the way it sells books. Webvan, the online grocery company, could get the hundreds of millions of dollars necessary to mount a credible challenge to existing grocery chains. This is the first economy, as Treasury Secretary Larry Summers says, "in which entrepreneurs may raise their first $100 million before buying their first suits."[6] That's what makes the New Economy new.

In the past, financial markets were good at funding large investments in physical capital by existing firms. But they could not cope with the high risk of new ventures, the high probabilities of failure, and the lack of collateral. Instead, much innovation was funded by existing large companies, which were often more concerned with protecting their existing markets than with opening up new ones. Radio Corporation of America (RCA), the preeminent high-tech company of the 1920s, was not a startup company. It was formed as a subsidiary of a British company and then bought by a group of big-company partners that included General Electric, AT&T, and Westinghouse, who were more interested in protecting their own interests than they were in pushing forward broadcast technology.[7]

Today, an RCA—and many competitors—would have been able to get funding from any number of venture capital firms. It would have been able to sell its stock on the stock market to raise the funds for expansion. It would have been able to borrow the funds it needed for its broadcast networks from sophisticated bankers. It would have been able to draw on a pool of skilled workers ready and willing to take a chance on a new business, in exchange for a piece of the action in the form of stock options.

Without this capacity to fund new and innovative businesses, the whole information revolution would have proceeded much more slowly. The technology was important, but alone it was not enough. Companies such as Intel, Apple, Oracle, Cisco, Netscape, and Amazon were able to grow explosively in large part because they all received venture capital funding in their early days. They could then expand quickly by drawing on the broader stock market.

This is why America has dominated the New Economy. Other countries have access to the same technology as the U.S., but they have lagged behind because they have been unable to duplicate the risk-taking capabilities of the American system of market-based funding of innovation.

In recent years, the effects of market-based funding of innovation have reached beyond the high-tech sector to embrace virtually every industry. Health care, grocery stores, insurance, financial services, utilities—every corner of the economy is experiencing competition from new venture-funded firms. The result is that existing companies are being forced to adopt innovations at an accelerated pace—whether they want to or not. They have to invest more to keep up, and they have to hold down prices if they want to compete. Productivity soars, inflation stays low, and the economy keeps expanding rapidly.

THE TECH CYCLE

So what's the problem? It's this: for the first time, the process of technological and business innovation amplifies the normal rhythms of the overall economy. Funding for innovation now depends on the state of the stock market and the expected growth of the country's gross domestic product (GDP). Technology has become synchronized with the ups and downs of the rest of the economy.

The result is that the Old Economy business cycle has been replaced by the New Economy *tech cycle:* longer expansions, followed by deeper and harsher recessions. On the upside, innovation and economic growth reinforce each other. More money spent on innovation means faster growth with low inflation. Faster growth and a rising stock market increase the incentives to invest in innovation—which yields more startups, faster adoption of technology, and more pressure on existing companies to keep up.

But when a downturn starts, watch out. The powerful forces that have made the New Economy so dynamic will begin moving in reverse—first slowly, then faster and faster. Rather than being led by housing and autos, as in the past, the next recession will be driven by the innovative sectors of the economy. A falling stock market and a slowing economy will mean lower potential payoffs even from successful startups, which will diminish the willingness of venture capitalists and corporations to put resources into the risky business of developing new innovations. The number of startups will decline, the pace of innovation will slow, and prices for tech equipment will fall more slowly or even start to rise, reducing the willingness of companies to buy new technology.

What's worse, as the wave of innovation slows, existing companies will lose their fear of being overrun by new competitors. With less pressure from rivals, and facing slower productivity growth and a squeeze on profit margins, any increase in wages will immediately translate into higher prices. Inflation will jump back in every sector of the economy.

Hardest hit, of course, will be the stock market. Rather than suffer a single sharp crash, the market will sour over time. The leading-edge Internet companies will tumble even farther than they did in the spring of 2000. Initial public offerings (IPOs) will come to a dead halt, and the downdraft will spread to the technology stocks, which accounted for roughly 45% of the gain in market value during the New Economy boom. Attempts by investors to pull their money out of the market will drive down stock prices even farther. Add in rising inflation and a slump in business investment, and stock prices could easily give back a substantial portion of the 200% gains they registered since 1995.

Some of the most lauded features of the New Economy will come back to haunt us. When venture capital dries up, so will the multitude of jobs being funded by it. The young college and business-school graduates who joined the dot.com revolution hoping for a quick score will be back living with their parents. Stock options will become worthless pieces of paper.

The unemployment rate will soar, affecting people who never expected to be out of work. Almost 60% of the new jobs generated between 1995 and 2000 were managerial or professional jobs, and these will be hit hard by the tech cycle downturn. The biggest cuts will happen among the people most intimately associated with the New Economy—the web site designers, the marketers at dot.coms, the consultants and investment bankers who rode the boom, and the journalists who covered them. The shortages of information technology (IT) workers—will turn into surpluses.

For a while the pain will be covered up. Some laid-off workers will switch to jobs at more traditional companies, while others will pay their bills with their credit cards. But eventually the downturn will spread to Old Economy companies as well, and the out-of-work will reach their credit limits. The $4 trillion in debt taken on by businesses and consumers in the past five years—the largest debt binge in U.S. history—will lead to a wave of bankruptcies and cutbacks in consumer spending. Stores and web sites will be filled with goods that no one can afford to buy. The damage is likely to spread globally as well. A slow-growth, high-inflation, tech-driven downturn in the U.S. could trigger an international financial crisis of historic proportions. For the past decade the U.S. has been sustaining global demand, accounting for more than half of the growth of the industrial economies in 1999 and absorbing much of the world's excess production of goods. At the same time, the flow of money into the U.S. has been astronomical, as foreign investors seek to benefit from the high returns produced by the boom. An economic slowdown in the U.S. could pull down growth in other countries, and trigger a massive outflow of capital. The potential outcome could be a witch's brew of soaring inflation, a plummeting dollar, and a sinking global economy.

THE THREAT OF DEPRESSION

The deterioration of the U.S. economy will not happen overnight. The protective institutions put in place in the 1930s will mean that there will be no banking panic, no wholesale closing of factories, no moment where it feels like the economy is in free fall. Even once the slowdown begins to broaden and deepen, it could take a year or two for the U.S. to actually slip into recession.

That's bad enough. But if policymakers don't respond quickly and aggressively to the unfolding tech downturn, there's a good chance that it could morph into something deeper and more sinister—an Internet Depression that drains the economy of its vigor for an extended period.

It's instructive to look back at the events of 1929 and 1930. It took about a year after the October 1929 stock market crash before businesses and investors realized that they were not simply in a mild decline. In the aftermath of the crash, the market actually rebounded, and for much of April 1930 the Standard and Poor's index was up on a year-over-year basis.

Similarly, it took at least a year before the effects of the 1990 Japanese stock market collapse percolated through that nation's economy. The Nikkei index peaked at the end of 1989 and then dropped by as much as 50% in 1990, triggering a decade-long slump. But well into 1991—more than a year later—capital investment was still rising rapidly, inflation was accelerating, and the governor of the Bank of Japan was still talking about the strong economy. The unemployment rate, which had dropped as low as 2%, did not rise over 2.2% until late in 1992.

In both cases, policymakers were deceived by the apparent strength of the economy, and misunderstood the dangers they faced. Economic historians now agree that the Federal Reserve's tight money policies in the late 1920s and early 1930s turned a stock market crash and recession into the Great Depression. Similarly, an extended pattern of mistakes by the Bank of Japan helped turn the stock market crash there into a long-lasting depression.

Most economists have an almost religious faith in the power of the central bank to stop the U.S. from slipping into another depression. It is conventional wisdom that policymakers have learned the lesson of these past disasters, and will act to cut interest rates sharply when danger looms.

But conventional wisdom is wrong: the odds of a bad policy mistake are far higher than economists realize. As in the 1920s, the U.S. economy today has entered a period of great technological change, in which the new capabilities of the economy outrun the ability of existing institutions to respond. It takes time to recognize new problems and figure out how to deal with them. Until that happens, economies are prone to exceptional fluctuations and bad policy mistakes.

If the Old Economy was an automobile, the New Economy is

an airplane. In an automobile, if anything unexpected happens, the natural and correct response is to put on the brakes. But just as an airplane needs a certain airspeed in order to stay aloft, so the New Economy needs fast growth in order for high-risk investment in innovation to be worthwhile. And just as pilots have to learn how to deal with a stalled and falling plane by the counterintuitive maneuver of pointing the nose towards the ground and adding power, policymakers have to learn how to go against their instincts by cutting rates when productivity growth slows and inflation goes up. It's the only way to keep from crashing.

DECISIONS, DECISIONS

If the U.S. falls into an Internet Depression, what's the best strategy for business executives, investors, and consumers? The answer depends on how long the depression is going to last, which in turn will be determined by the response of policymakers.

If the Federal Reserve, Congress, and the White House all work together to counter the downturn, then it may be deep but relatively short. In that case, the correct strategy is to "buy on the dip," in the broadest sense. Businesses should keep investing in new technology under the assumption that their investments will pay off in the future. Investors should buy stocks as they get cheaper, under the assumption that they will shortly go up. Workers should continue to seek jobs in new companies in hot industries, and even accept stock options, under the assumption that growth in high-tech will resume. These optimistic strategies have been successful for the past decade or more.

But there is another, more distressing possibility. Both the Great Depression of the 1930s and the long Japanese slump of the 1990s lasted far longer than anyone thought possible. The Great Depression, by many accounts, didn't end until the U.S. got involved in World War II, and the Japanese slump is still not yet clearly over. Once capitalist economies break down, they are very hard to get running again.

If the U.S. economy gets stuck in a long Internet Depression, the appropriate strategy is to hunker down, cut back, and invest as conservatively as possible. That will be the only way to survive and be ready to take advantage of the end of the depression, whenever it comes.

The downturn could be not only the dominant economic event of the decade but also its major political event. If policymakers do not grasp the difference between driving a car and flying an airplane, the U.S. could be stuck in a long depression. At some point the recovery may require stronger measures than simply cutting interest rates and boosting spending. Just as the New Deal involved government intervention in the financial and labor markets in order to stabilize them, so government may have to take a hand in the high-tech sector to stabilize the New Economy. That's not politically feasible now, but it's worth remembering that the Great Depression did not end until the politicians and central bankers who were committed to misguided deflationary policies were replaced. "Countries only began the struggle to restore prosperity under new leadership," observe economic historians Barry Eichengreen and Peter Temin. It was only when mass politics removed the old leaders from power that the process of economy recovery could begin.[8]

OPTIMISTIC OR PESSIMISTIC?

Am I being too apocalyptic? Perhaps. After all, economic growth and spending on information technology were still barreling ahead in the first half of 2000. Growth in Europe and Japan seems to be slowly picking up. And while many economists still believe that the stock market is overvalued, none of the conventional macroeconomics forecasting models predict anything more than a mild recession, even if the market drops by 20%.

On the other hand, these same models completely failed to predict the boom of the 1990s. Nobody has ever seen how Amazon.com, eBay, or any of the deregulated telephone companies behave in a real tech recession. Nobody knows how an economy built on information technology and rapid innovation will react to a sharp downturn. We are entering uncharted territory—and here be dragons.

CHAPTER TWO

What's New about the New Economy

IT'S NEARLY IMPOSSIBLE to identify the day on which a new economic era dawns. But you can make a good case that the New Economy was born in the U.S. on August 9, 1995.[1] That was the day that Netscape, the Internet browser company now part of America Online, went public. To much fanfare, the price of Netscape stock, initially set at $28 per share, more than doubled by the end of the day. The stock kept soaring, making fortunes for early investors and setting off an Internet frenzy that lasted for over five years.

From that point on, it was as if the U.S. had transformed itself into a different economy. Clark Kent turned into Superman, without even needing a phone booth. Growth and productivity accelerated, inflation and unemployment fell. There was virtually no economic measure that did not improve (see Table 2.1).[2]

Why was the Netscape IPO a turning point? It was not simply a signal that the Internet was for real, although that was very important. Nor was it simply a sign that there was big money to be made in the stock market, although that was important too.

Rather, a company that had not existed two years earlier was

Table 2.1   The Netscape Difference

	Before Netscape IPO[a]	After Netscape IPO[b]
GDP growth rate	3.0%	4.3%
Nonfarm productivity growth rate	1.7%	2.8%
Unemployment rate	6.6%	4.8%
Core inflation	3.3%	2.3%

Sources: Bureau of Labor Statistics; Bureau of Economic Analysis; author calculations.

[a]Annual rate, measured from the beginning of the expansion in the first quarter of 1991 to the third quarter of 1995.

[b]Annual rate, measured from the third quarter of 1995 to the first quarter of 2000.

challenging the largest and most powerful software company in the world, Microsoft, and its leader, Bill Gates. And Gates responded by putting his company into hyperdrive. He greatly sped up development of its web browser Internet Explorer, and then bundled it for free with Windows. As Gates proudly told analysts, customers, and reporters at a conference in December 1995, the "sleeping giant" had awakened.

The aftermath of the Netscape IPO set the pattern for the New Economy: increased competition, accelerating technological change, no inflation. Over the next four years, in industry after industry, an onslaught of startups forced existing firms to move faster, adopt new technology, and cut prices. Amazon.com came in and attacked Barnes and Noble, eToys attacked Toys "Я" Us, E*Trade attacked Merrill Lynch.

The key in every case was the same: cutting-edge Internet technology plus the financing to mount a credible challenge. Unlike any other country, America had a vigorous venture capital industry that was not just willing but committed to financing innovative startups. Unlike any other country, America had pension funds, university endowments, and other large institutional investors not just willing but anxious to channel their money into venture firms that funded new businesses. And unlike any other country, America had a vibrant IPO market not just willing but eager to buy shares in the businesses of the future.

Venture capital sustained Netscape until it could go public, and then the proceeds from the public offering turned Netscape into a serious threat to Microsoft. That the startup was well-funded made all the difference in the world to the seriousness of Microsoft's reaction.[3] The same was true for the rest of the startups as well. Technology was the engine, finance was the fuel.

The usual notion that the New Economy has been driven by technology and globalization is incomplete. In fact, the economic performance of the 1990s would simply not have been possible without access to capital—and not just any money, but money that was interested in funding new businesses with innovative ideas. Without access to capital, the Internet Age would have arrived, but much more slowly. Online businesses would have been created, but often as subsidiaries of existing companies with a consumer franchise to protect. E-commerce would have arrived and the economy would have grown, but much more slowly. And the U.S. would have had a half-New Economy rather than a whole one.

From this perspective, the astonishing rise in the stock market in the 1990s was not simply a sideshow to the real action. Rather, the financial markets were an essential part of the machinery driving innovation and productivity forward. With the possibility of big gains from innovation, the incentives changed to make it much more profitable to invest in high-risk new businesses.

The importance of the new set of financial institutions that made this investment possible—extensive networks of well-financed venture capital firms, deep and liquid stock markets able to absorb IPOs, and the availability of stock options to motivate workers—cannot be overstated. The Old Economy marshaled the forces of the financial markets to support investment in physical capital, such as factories, railroads, and roads. The New Economy marshals the forces of the financial markets to support innovation—and that's a big difference.

THE ROLE OF FINANCIAL MARKETS

A critical part of any industrial or technological revolution is the creation of new financial institutions. The modern stock and bond markets did not exist until they were triggered by the financing needs of the railroads in the second half of the 1800s. Railroads required mammoth amounts of capital to build, far more than any previous nongovernment operations. The total investment in American railroads came to roughly $10 billion in 1890[4]—an enormous sum at a time when the entire annual output of the economy was on the order of $13 billion.

Such large amounts of money could not be raised from local banks or from the tiny stock and bond markets that existed at the time. Instead, capital from all over the country and Europe was funneled through New York City, creating the first truly national stock and bond markets, the first modern underwriting syndicates for bonds, and the first modern investment banking firms (not to mention the first modern stock swindles).

The railroads were not the only beneficiaries of the new financial markets. The U.S. now possessed, for the first time, credit markets capable of funding large-scale capital investments on a national scale. This greatly accelerated the industrialization and expansion of the U.S. economy in the early part of the 20th century. When capital-intensive companies such as the electric utilities and the automobile makers needed to grow, they had easy access to capital.

By comparison, innovation has until fairly recently been difficult to finance within the normal framework of the market economy. The modern stock and bond markets have historically been extremely good at funneling large sums of money to capital-intensive industries such as railroads, utilities, and large industrial enterprises. These industries all had relatively steady cash flows and physical assets that could be used as collateral if something went wrong.

By contrast, banks and capital markets simply had no good way of financing small, innovative firms. The risks of providing money to a startup company with no track record were simply too high, and the odds of success were too low. Lenders and investors had no way of knowing if there was a market for the product or service, if it would do what it was supposed to, or if it could be sold cheaply enough. Economic history is littered with supposedly good ideas that simply did not find an audience. As management expert Peter Drucker wrote:

> No one can tell in advance whether the user is going to be receptive, indifferent, or actively resistant. . . . In most knowledge-based innovations, receptivity is a gamble. And the odds are unknown, are indeed mysterious. . . . There is no way to eliminate the element of risk, no way even to reduce it.[5]

Moreover, a new company usually had few physical assets, providing lenders with no collateral and no recourse if the company went under. That fact alone would discourage most lenders. From this perspective, the American-style venture capital fund is one of the great financial breakthroughs of the 20th century.

THE RISE OF THE VENTURE CAPITAL ECONOMY

Economists have generally sneered at venture capital as being too small to notice. In 1988, the peak year for venture capital in the 1980s, the amount dispersed was just over $5 billion. By comparison, total U.S. spending on research and development (R&D) in that same year was $134 billion.

In the 1980s, venture capital also suffered from the general bias against high-tech companies, which seemed like toys next to the giants of the Old Economy. In 1989, Intel had only $3 billion in sales, compared to $124 billion for a "real" company like General Motors. Microsoft was a pip-squeak with only $800 million in revenues. The Nasdaq stock exchange, where many of the startups went public, was held in disdain by Wall Street.

But that time is over. Beyond any doubt, venture capital is the fastest-growing part of the financial system. In 1999, venture capital firms dispersed $48 billion to new startups. In the first quarter of 2000, venture capital funding was running at roughly a $90 billion annual rate.

Looking at the excellent returns on venture capital makes it clear why it has grown so quickly. The annual rate of return on venture capital over the past twenty years is running at about 16%, substantially higher than other investments. Venture capital has an edge even after adjusting for risk. One study showed that venture capital earns a return 7% to 10% higher than public stocks with similar risk.[6]

Venture capital has increased to the point where it rivals R&D as a source of funding for innovation. In the first quarter of 2000 it equaled fully one-third of all money spent on R&D, compared to an average of 3% in the 1980s (see Figure 2.1).

The social impact of venture capital may be even larger than these numbers show. One 1998 study calculated that a dollar of venture capital stimulates 3 to 5 times more patents than a dollar of corporate R&D spending.[7] Taking patents as a rough measure of innovation, the current surge of venture capital funding, if it continues, could generate as much innovation as all of corporate R&D spending added together.

What makes venture capital so potent? Venture capital, on the

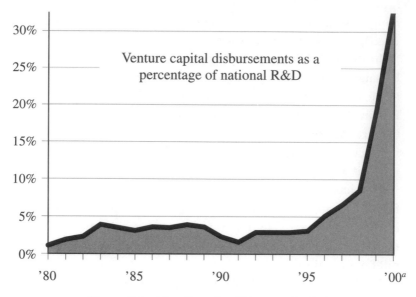

Figure 2.1   The Growth of Venture Capital

Sources: National Venture Capital Association; National Science Foundations.
[a]Estimated, based on first quarter only.

face of it, looks simple: a limited partnership organized for the purpose of investing in new and innovative businesses. But, in fact, venture capitalists are only the tip of a large and sophisticated capital system that is capable of absorbing and diffusing the large amounts of risk necessary to fund startups and young companies.

The first organized venture capital firm was American Research and Development, founded in 1946 by a group that included a professor at Harvard Business School and the president of the Federal Reserve Bank of Boston. Their goal was to ensure that the technologies developed during the war would find applications in the private sector. The firm's big initial success story was investing $70,000 in a new company formed by four MIT graduate students. That company later became Digital Equipment Corporation, a successful maker of minicomputers, and the original investment turned into several hundred million dollars.[8]

Soon thereafter, the venture capital industry took root in Silicon Valley, where it helped create the high-tech industry we know today. Even before the latest surge of spending, venture capital was instrumental in the startup of some of the biggest names in information technology and biotechnology, including Apple Computer, Intel, Lotus, Sun, Compaq, and Genetech.

An essential part of the Silicon Valley mystique revolves around the formation of new businesses, starting with the story of three engineers who left Fairchild Camera and Instrument Corporation in 1968, and with $2 million raised by venture capitalist Arthur Rock, started Intel, the first company to introduce a programmable microprocessor. No one is saying that the microprocessor would not have been invented without Intel—but it would have developed much more slowly.

The venture capital firms are only one part of the equation. Three other key elements are needed to make the system work. The first is institutional investors with very deep pockets and a willingness to take risks. About 40% of the money put up for venture capital funds in the 1990s came from public and private pension funds, with another 15% coming from college endowments, foundations, and similar organizations. The involvement of pension funds in the venture capital business dates back to 1978, when a revision of the "prudent man" rule allowed pension fund managers to invest in risky assets such as venture capital. As of April 2000, the largest public pension fund in the country, California's Calpers, had 3.7% of its assets, or $6.4 billion, in private equity (which includes venture capital).

The second essential part of the venture process is the IPO, which serves several purposes. First, the lure of a successful IPO provides powerful incentives for workers and managers, who generally hold stock options, to devote themselves to the startup. It provides funds for expansion, and enables venture capital investors to cash out without waiting ten or twenty years, and to recycle the money back into other ventures. Finally, the IPO provides a critical link between venture capitalists and broader market forces. In their study of financial systems, economists Raghuram R. Rajan and Luigi Zingales of the University of Chicago note that "the need to exit via the market ensures that prices eventually do matter and discipline the investments that take place."[9]

The final critical piece of the risk capital system is a pool of entrepreneurial, educated, and creative workers willing and able to take risks. Not permanently wedded to any existing company, they form a mobile attack force that can flow to the companies and projects that have the greatest chance of a breakthrough. In many ways, this is what countries such as Germany and Japan lack. Their most competent people have traditionally had well-paying, prestigious jobs at large corporations with more security than Americans had—and if they ever left these jobs to start a company, their former employer would never hire them back again.

In the U.S., the widespread use of stock options as a major form of compensation is a key part of the New Economy. It means that managers and workers have a major incentive to not walk away from their startup until it has gone through a successful IPO. That aligns their interests with those of the venture capitalists and provides a substitute for the lack of physical collateral. This turns the labor market, for the first time, into an extension of the financial system.

THE AMERICAN EDGE

Why did the New Economy start in the U.S., rather than in Japan or Europe? After all, Japan and Germany began the 1990s with almost as a good a technology base as the U.S. had, by most accounts, and in some areas better. They invested more in civilian R&D as a share of GDP than the U.S. did. Japan's manufacturing capabilities in such crucial technologies as memory chips and LCD screens were thought to be second to none.

Moreover, the U.S. was the *least* globalized of all the major industrial countries. In 1995, exports of goods and services amounted to about 11% of U.S. GDP. By comparison, in countries such as Germany, France, the United Kingdom, and even Italy, exports were on the order of 25% of GDP. In some ways, these countries were all much better positioned to take advantage of a growing world economy, since their companies were already more oriented toward global markets.

The U.S. did have the advantages of early deregulation and a more flexible labor market. But more important, what the U.S. had that the other countries didn't was a system capable of financing and nurturing innovative activity and the creation of new businesses. In a word, it was driven by a higher-powered engine, capable of producing more ideas and turning them into real products and real companies faster.

America's competitors could see what they lacked. Germany, Great Britain, and Japan tried for decades to develop venture capital industries, with little success. In Germany, for example, the first venture capital firms were started in the 1960s by banks, but they inherited the caution of their parent corporations and did not invest in new, small firms.[10] Another attempt in the 1970s to encourage venture capital, this time by the German government, failed as well. Yet more venture capital firms were started in the 1980s, but their technology investments were spectacularly unsuccessful. As a result, notes one set of researchers, "these firms were no longer supplying any risk-sustaining capital worth mentioning after 1989".[11]

The experience was similar in the United Kingdom, where a wave of British venture capital firms opened their doors in the late 1970s and early 1980s. But they quickly turned from financing startups to financing management buyouts of existing firms.

By 1991, only 6% of the total venture capital funds invested were going to startups or early-stage financings.[12]

Why did these non-U.S. venture capital industries keep failing to reach their goals? First, in many countries there was a shortage of workers willing to step outside the safe confines of large corporations. Moreover, a well-functioning IPO market that gives early investors a way to cash out is not an easy thing to put in place. There has to be a broad and deep equity market willing to buy up shares of a growing young business in its difficult adolescent stage—big enough to venture out into the wide world, but young enough that the future of the business is not assured.[13]

The late 1990s saw the beginning of vibrant IPO markets outside the U.S., accompanied by an emerging venture capital industry. In Europe the new growth stock markets, the Euro.NM and Easdaq, finally started getting big enough and liquid enough to be attractive as places to take a company public. Hong Kong opened up a new market for listing high-tech companies in the fall of 1999, and countries such as India and Japan started getting into the act. But it remains to be seen whether any of these markets have a sufficient depth of capital to keep functioning when times turn bad.

WHY RISK CAPITAL MAKES A DIFFERENCE

The New Economy, as we've seen, has performed far better than the Old Economy—lower inflation, lower unemployment, faster growth, stronger productivity gains. In fact, it has performed better than many economists thought possible. If these measures mean anything at all, they are telling us that the New Economy is somehow able to use its resources more effectively than the Old. What exactly has improved?

Profit-making

One of the biggest advantages of venture capital is that it is single-minded in pursuit of financial returns. Venture capitalists are not trying to protect existing products and markets, as big companies do, nor do they worry about national security or local economic development. As a result, money is directed toward the ventures with the highest expected payoffs. That's a good recipe for speeding up innovation.

Now let's be very clear. Venture capital responds only to the highest *private* returns to investors. It does not and cannot replace basic research, which has no immediate profit-making application. Almost by definition, basic research needs to be funded outside the market system, by the government, universities, and similar institutions. In fact, as we will see in Chapter 9, there's a good argument that the continued health of the New Economy and the venture capital industry depends on increased government spending on basic research and education.

Nevertheless, venture capital funds are unique in economic history. No other institutions—ever—were devoted exclusively to assessing and funding innovation for pure profit reasons. Government support for R&D, of course, has been mainly focused on national security and support for basic research. And universities, by and large, are intentionally not designed to steer research toward the most profitable opportunities. One of the main justifications of a research university is to allow faculty the freedom to follow basic research that has no immediate commercial application. While universities are more attuned these days to extracting some monetary benefit from the ideas generated in campus labs, that's still not the main purpose of the institution.

More surprisingly, it's also become clear that most corporations—which account for 75% of total R&D spending—have a conflicted attitude toward new ideas. Certainly large companies can be a powerful source of innovation, as IBM, General Electric, and AT&T have shown. Ideas that either improve the usefulness or lower the cost of existing products get the green light. And companies are more than willing to spend heavily to develop new products, if they can identify an unmet need among their existing customers.

But the breakthrough ideas—the ones that have the potential to create whole new markets, perhaps with new customers, new distribution channels, and a new way of operating—have a much harder time finding support within most big companies. This was the main point of Clayton Christensen's groundbreaking 1997 book, *The Innovator's Dilemma,* which argued that big companies have great difficulty taking advantage of what Christensen calls "disruptive innovations."

Corporate executives quite naturally do not like failure—and the essence of disruptive innovation is that there are lots of failures. Writes Christensen:

> Individual managers in most organizations believe that . . . if they champion a project that fails because the initial marketing plan was wrong, it will constitute a blotch on their track record, blocking their rise through the organization. . . . Most individual decision makers find it very difficult to risk backing a project that might fail because the market is not there.[14]

But with disruptive innovations, markets and profits are never guaranteed.

What is also missing from most corporate R&D is the accelerated leap from idea to breakthrough product market that characterizes today's Internet economy. Corporate executives have to worry about whether a new product or service is going to cannibalize sales of existing products. That means they are often more concerned with "managing the pace" of innovation—code words for slowing it down—than with encouraging it. IBM, for example, fell behind in the PC race because it kept trying to pro-

tect its profitable mainframe businesses. As a result, it introduced the laughable PCjr in 1984, with its chiclet-like keyboard,
rather than following up the success of the original IBM PC. It's
natural for large corporations to decide that protecting their
existing profit streams is more important than taking a chance
on an unproven product.

Diversification

Another benefit of the venture-based system driving the U.S. New
Economy is that it promotes diversification and experimentation.
In practice, most large companies only have limited funds available for new projects, which must compete against existing needs
and programs. Within that limited pool, there is usually an internal political need to put most of the available resources into projects that fit the corporation's "strategic vision."

But, in fact, the process of identifying innovative ideas that
actually work is like drilling for oil—it may be necessary to dig a
lot of holes before finding a gusher. A study of venture capital
investments made between 1969 and 1985 showed that more
than one-third ended in a loss; only 7% had payoffs greater than
10 times the original cost.[15] Even during the late 1990s, when the
percentage of big successes was much higher, plenty of venture
startups simply fizzled out or were sold to other companies at
relatively low prices.

That's why almost all venture capital funds carry large port-
folios of companies. A major venture capital fund may be
invested at any time in upwards of fifty to one hundred new
companies—and this sort of diversification and experimentation increases the chance of uncovering a winner.

Many of the biggest Internet successes would not have made
it through a "sensible" corporate planning process. For example, when eBay first started out in 1995, few people would have
predicted that online auctions would be such a big hit. But eBay,
funded by venture firm Benchmark Capital, was allowed to grow

until it reached critical mass. There was virtually no interest or attention until eBay went public in September 1998, then almost overnight it became one of the most visited sites on the Web.

Similarly, some of the biggest successes of biotechnology might not have been funded if they had been part of a large corporation and had to compete for money against more mainstream internal projects. The biotech startup Amgen, for example, was struggling before it scored big with drugs to boost the production of red and white blood cells. But as one author notes, "Amgen's original business plan called for programs in chicken and pig growth hormone—its fabulously successful products Epogen and Neupogen weren't even imagined in the old days."[16]

Weeding

Paradoxically, venture capitalists not only fund more projects, they are also better at weeding out the losing ones. Venture capital money is doled out in stages, and at every point along the way the odds of success are reassessed. And because venture capitalists are funding multiple companies simultaneously, they don't get too emotionally invested in any single one. By not putting more money into losing bets, they can afford to fund a lot more ideas.

The result is a system that makes far better use of its resources, and consequently produces many more successful startups. William Sahlman, a professor at the Harvard Business School, told the *Boston Globe* in February 2000, "I think we have increased the chance of commercial success by a factor of five or six."[17] Studies suggest that companies backed by venture capital perform better on several business and financial dimensions, including post-IPO stock performance and speed of products to market.[18]

It becomes much harder for corporations and governments to pull the plug on bad ideas, once they have developed sufficient momentum. New initiatives develop a constituency, people's careers become tied to them, and they can keep going longer than a rational analysis would justify.

One famous example is the Iridium satellite system, which was intended to offer worldwide cellular service. Motorola, the main company sponsoring the project, announced its plans for Iridium in 1990 to a blaze of publicity. But Motorola's commitment of corporate prestige and resources to the project made it tough to acknowledge growing doubts about the economics of Iridium. By the time that the sixty-six-satellite system went operational in late 1998, at a cost of $5 billion, much of the world was covered by ground-based cellular telephone service. Moreover, the satellite phones were expensive and did not function as well as a good cell phone in most locations. There was no demand, and the company took a quick trip into bankruptcy.

Paradoxically, the difficulty of shutting projects down actually reduces the amount of funding available. Governments and corporations have to be cautious about funding new initiatives for fear of creating a vested interest and a monetary sinkhole. The result is far less innovative activity.

Management

One of the more subtle advantages of the venture capital system is the ability to help a young company make the jump from revenue-free startup to profitable operating company. In part, venture capitalists do this by offering their advice and contacts to young firms. Sponsorship by a top-tier venture capital firm can open doors and make it easier to get topflight managers.

But venture capital firms do something else: they closely monitor the performance of the startup, and step in if necessary. Most venture investments are written with provisions that give venture capitalists either control over the board of the startup or veto power over major operating decisions. In the extreme case, venture capitalists can replace the founder of a struggling company with an outside CEO. That's an important element in the success of many venture-based firms.

But the U.S. venture capital system is based on a delicate balance: too much control by investors would destroy the incentives for entrepreneurs, who are often driven to start companies because they like running their own operations. So generally venture capital investments are written in such a way that they give more control to entrepreneurs when the company does well.[19] A successful IPO almost invariably wipes out any special rights that venture capitalists have.

ACCELERATION OF TECHNOLOGICAL CHANGE

Economists like to think technology evolves at a more or less steady rate. As engineers and scientists labor behind the scenes, their eyes fixed on higher concerns than money or commerce, the economy's "production possibility frontier" is steadily pushed out through good times and bad.

That may be true to the extent that research in university or government laboratories is insulated from the ups and downs of the economy. But in the real world, money matters. You can have the best idea in the world—one capable of creating a new Intel or Amazon.com—but unless you can get the money you need to develop it and bring it to market, it will get no farther than your desk drawer.

The funding of ideas through the financial markets means both technological and business innovation is accelerated. New ideas and new business models can move quickly from the laboratory, the workbench, or somebody's head into the real world without being filtered through a corporation's or a government's preconceived notion of what makes sense. Anything that looks like it might be profitable gets funded.

This is especially advantageous in an era when the rules are changing and the winning approach is not clear. Venture capital provides the means to fund multiple simultaneous experiments. If one startup doesn't work, another will. Harnessed to the profit motive, the resources of a rich country are efficiently employed to explore a wide range of alternative business models and technological possibilities.

In that sense, the speed at which new ideas are introduced into the economy is very much linked to the availability of financing. Easier funding means that more ideas and innovations can be tested in the market, which means that the ones which work can be identified sooner and adopted faster. Stronger stock markets mean easier funding and quicker adoption, tighter funding means slower adoption. At the top of the tech cycle, ideas leap from the drawing board into practice seemingly overnight.

In the past few years, the amount of money flowing into the venture capital system has increased to the point where even expensive but potentially quite important ideas can be tested. Consider the grocery store–based system of food distribution, an enormous but troubled industry that has actually experienced falling productivity in recent years.[20] Having a viable online alternative that did not require shoppers to spend so many hours pushing carts through cavernous stores and standing in checkout lines seemed to have the potential of making a big economic impact.

The new financial markets were willing to finance not just one but several online food delivery companies, each one an extremely capital-intensive operation. Webvan, the leading online grocery delivery service, was able to raise roughly $800 million in 1998 and 1999, combining venture capital funding and its November 1999 IPO. As of mid-2000, it had rolled out its delivery service in several cities, with more to come.

Online grocery shopping may or may not turn out to be a more efficient business model than current grocery stores. Webvan itself may succeed or fail. Indeed, the stock price of Webvan fell sharply in early 2000, as investors started to have doubts about the viability of the online grocery store. But without the availability of risk capital, this alternative business model could not even have been tried.

Venture funding also spurs the development of new tools and technologies that existing companies can adapt to their own purposes. In February 2000, for example, General Motors and Ford (later joined by DaimlerChrysler) announced their plans for an online trading exchange linking auto suppliers with automakers, potentially covering up to $250 billion in purchases. One of the two main companies setting up the exchange was Commerce One, a startup that had received roughly $50 million in venture and private equity funding since its founding in 1997. Without this funding, there is no way that Commerce One would have been ready for a project of this magnitude.

Even if small startup companies don't become big successes, they are a source of new ideas that can be absorbed into larger companies. That's one critical way for large firms to manage the high risk of early-stage new product development. Established drug companies, for example, may take big stakes in biotechnology companies, buy rights to drugs developed at the smaller companies, or even buy whole companies.

Another master of this technique is Cisco, which has thrived by acquiring and absorbing small companies with cutting-edge technologies. In the first half of 2000 alone, Cisco announced twelve acquisitions, most of which were originally venture-funded. In essence, Cisco was using venture capital as an indirect means of funding its R&D efforts.

COMPETITION AND INVESTMENT

One of the distinguishing features of the New Economy, at least so far, is the intense competitive pressure that companies face.

Part of that comes from globalization, which means that U.S. manufacturers are exposed to both the threat of foreign competition and the lure of foreign markets. Both can serve to boost productivity. Writes one economist,

> On the import side, an increase in imports can show firms what new varieties of products are available, and reverse engineering can communicate new technologies. . . . On the export side, simply committing to try to export can encourage technological uptake and best practice.[21]

The increased globalization of the U.S. economy in the 1980s and 1990s played an important role in the pickup of manufacturing productivity.

Technology has the same effect. When a new technology such as the Internet arrives, it creates more competition. Costs fall, and established firms find themselves facing more competition from a variety of sources. And the effects go far beyond the high-tech industries.

Stir in funding for new startups, and the competitive pressure goes white-hot. The existence of venture capitalists willing to back upstarts produces a "racehorse" effect. It creates viable competitors to existing businesses and forces them to think like venture capitalists as well. Even the most reluctant companies are forced to innovate or face being left behind. As entrepreneurship expert William Sahlman wrote in the *Harvard Business Review* in 1999:

> That is what the new economy is all about—companies attacking the status quo and entrenched players, and experimenting to find new technologies that improve or replace earlier ones. . . . Sectors that once seemed impervious to systematic improvement are also under assault—for the better.[22]

Would Microsoft have poured so much money and effort into its Internet projects if the pressure from Netscape and other startups had not been there? It would have been a lot more tempting for Microsoft to encourage people to join its own proprietary online service in which it had invested heavily. A large faction in Microsoft certainly favored that strategy.

Or look at the race to map the human genome. The Human Genome Project, funded with government and nonprofit money, had originally set a leisurely date of 2005 for delivering the human genome sequence. But under pressure from a private venture-funded competitor, the Human Genome Project was forced to move up its schedule several times.[23] In the end, most of the human genome was announced in the spring of 2000, years earlier than expected. Part of that speedup came from improvements in technology, but part was simply the threat of being left behind.

The threat of competition also forces existing companies to invest more in their own business. In an era of rapid technological change, there is another strong incentive to invest—fear. Brick-and-mortar companies were petrified that a dot.com would spring up and undercut them. As a result, existing businesses spent big bucks to set up web sites, even if there was no immediate way these investments could make money.

For example, in 1999, Toys "Я" Us spent $86 million to set up its web site as a competitive response to eToys and other online toy retailers. The web site was by no means an initial success. nevertheless, this was money that the company would not have spent otherwise. Total capital spending for Toys "Я" Us in 1999 totaled $533 million, up 43% from the previous year.

To put it a different way, a rapid pace of innovation and the availability of capital force companies to look more toward the future. They are investing not simply to take advantage of today's technology, but to be in a position to take advantage of products and capabilities that don't even exist today. They are paying the entry fee to a race that may or may not be run, where the size of the final prizes is unknown and the number of contestants is not yet determined.

COMPETITION AND INFLATION

In 1982, William Baumol, an economist at Princeton University at the time (and now on the short list of potential Nobel Prize winners), coined the term "contestable markets." This was the idea that price increases could be restrained by fear of new entrants: the greater the fear of potential competition, the less inflation.

The prototypical contestable market was originally supposed to be the airline industry. It turned out, however, that existing airlines had sufficient pricing leverage and power to keep out most new airlines. Moreover, it was difficult in most industries for new entrants to get the financing that would make them realistic competitors.

That changed in the New Economy. In the expansion phase of the tech cycle, rapid technological change and the availability of capital for startups turn virtually every industry into a contestable industry. Retailing, real estate, financial services, insurance, banking, media, software, hardware, grocery store chains, mammoth financial institutions: in virtually every industry, new competitors can come out of nowhere.

As long as the money keeps flowing to new businesses, there will plenty of pressure to keep prices low. This may be one reason why inflation stayed under control so long during the boom of the 1990s. When rapid growth is driven by technological change, it creates more opportunities for new entrants and puts more pressure on existing firms to hold down prices.

Competition is also reaching deep into areas of the economy where competition has traditionally been anathema. Real estate brokerage commissions, for instance, have long been resistant to change. But a plethora of online real estate brokers offering lower commissions or fixed fee deals have begun to drive down the price of real estate transactions.

The combination of both the new technology and the capital

for startups throws fear into existing companies and induces them to either hold down their price increases or to charge lower prices. For example, in June 1999, the threat of E*Trade, the low-cost Internet broker, forced Merrill Lynch, the largest brokerage firm in the country, to start an online service that let customers trade for a flat fee of $29.95 per transaction, much less than most of them had to pay before. Charles Schwab, the discount brokerage, had been charging a flat fee for much longer, but it wasn't until E*Trade showed up that Merrill was forced to cut its prices.

It's important to note that E*Trade posed a serious challenge to Merrill and the other Wall Street brokers only because it was able to raise large sums of money from venture capital firms, an IPO, and a secondary offering of stock. All told, these provided the base of capital that E*Trade needed to be a first-string competitor.

THE ROLE OF THE STOCK MARKET

The spectacular rise of the stock market in the 1990s has produced wildly different appraisals from economists. Pessimists such as Robert Shiller, an economist at Yale University and author of *Irrational Exuberance,* argue that the market is trapped in a speculative bubble. Optimists such as James Glassman and Kevin Hassett, authors of *Dow 36,000,* believe that equities are not as risky as people think, and that despite having nearly tripled between the beginning of 1995 and the end of 1999, the market is justified in going much higher.

Both sides miss the real point. The stock market is not simply an innocent bystander in the New Economy. Rather, with the rise of risk capital, the market has become the critical nexus of economic growth and innovation. Rising stock prices are not just a reflection of faster economic growth; rather, they are an essential component of the New Economy system for financing innovation and technological change. The prospect of going public at a high valuation is the carrot that spurs rapid innovation and risk-taking.

In effect, investors are treating the stock market—and the tech sector in particular—as a giant venture capital fund, with expectations of getting the same sorts of annual returns (15% to 20%) that venture capitalists get. That's enough to raise long-term growth rates for the economy and to justify higher prices for stocks. Shiller-type pessimism is unjustified because the new venture capital markets drive a self-reinforcing cycle of innovation, yielding a continuing stream of new companies and technological change.

But there's a catch. Investors are not just betting on the profits from today's companies selling today's products and services. If they were, they wouldn't be willing to give enormous market values to companies that have no way of showing a profit. Instead, they bet on companies that have not yet been created, and innovations that have not yet been conceived of.

The essence of the New Economy is the extension of the equity markets to *riskier* investments. More and more people are heavily invested in volatile technology companies. Many of these companies are only a few years old and have never shown any profits—the very definition of risky. And there is no guarantee of any profits in the future.

It may be true, as Glassman and Hassett argue, that Old Economy stocks are less risky than investors have historically believed. But Americans are increasingly willing to take bigger risks to get bigger returns. It's this willingness to take unprecedented risks—to support with cold cash not only the unproven but even the unthought-of—that ultimately drives the New Economy.

Technology and globalization are essential, but risk capital gives the extra jolt that turns decent economic growth into something special: faster innovation, lower inflation, and an almost palpable sense of excitement. The waves of innovation come closer and closer together until they are almost a single torrent. The result is a higher long-term rate of growth, and a better future for us and our kids. But as we will see, gains from turbocharging the economy do not come without a price.

CHAPTER THREE

The Last Depression

THE GREAT DEPRESSION resonates in our collective memory like a dimly remembered nervous breakdown, inexplicable and horrifying. It started slowly, but the economy kept slipping further and further into a nightmarish derangement unprecedented in scope, scale, and depth. "Like a plague, the disease of deprivation spread with such speed and across so many lines that there were few families who did not experience or witness its pain."[1]

The four years from the top of the boom in 1929 to the bottom of the Depression in 1933 were like an eternity in one sense, and an eyeblink in another. In 1933, when one-quarter of the labor force was unemployed, a return to the good years seemed as unlikely as a trip to the moon. Yet Frederick Allen called his classic history of the Depression years *Only Yesterday* because it felt as if the bad years were separated from the boom of the 1920s only by the thin line that distinguishes shadow from light.

The good news is that an industrial depression is unlikely to happen again. The kind of widespread destitution that many older Americans still remember will not return. The ability of consumers to spend is supported by Social Security, unemployment insurance, Medicare and Medicaid, and a large defense budget. Government spending takes up a much larger share of the economy and provides an anchor that did not exist in the Great Depression. The financial sector is buttressed by deposit insurance and regulations that will prevent people from panicking and trying to withdraw all their money from banks, thus eliminating the sort of bank runs that made the Depression so terrifying. Most important, the U.S. has a central bank that understands the appropriate response to an incipient industrial depression or a financial panic. People and governments keep making mistakes, as Nobel Prize–winning economist Milton Friedman observed in 1995, "but after a point they stop making the same mistakes."[2]

Still, the analogies are disquieting, since the era that most closely resembles the present in its combination of financial and technological innovation is the 1920s. That boom was rooted in the rise of the automobile, fueled by a rising stock market and wide open consumer credit. As in the 1990s, Americans had the utmost confidence in both the superiority of the American economy and the ability of the Federal Reserve to steer it. But as one historian wrote,

> The people running the economic machinery simply did not fully understand the system they were operating. Official dependence on outdated cliches—such as maintaining the gold standard, balancing the budget, and opposing inflation—all posed insuperable barriers to an early solution to the crisis.[3]

It was policy mistakes by the Federal Reserve that turned a garden-variety recession into a depression.

TECHNOLOGY AND FINANCE UNITED

The automobile was the preeminent technological innovation of the 20th century. Just as information technology has driven the boom of the 1990s, the boom of the 1920s was driven by the automobile industry and its suppliers. More than 31 million cars were produced in the 1920s, in a country with less than 30 million households. Steel, rubber, and glass companies built plants to meet the voracious needs of the automakers, oil companies dug wells and put up filling stations, construction crews laid roads, and developers built homes that could only be reached by the new automobiles.

But it wasn't simply technology that created the auto boom. The invention and widespread acceptance of consumer installment credit made it possible for millions of middle- and lower-class Americans to buy cars. For the first time, consumers could borrow for large purchases such as automobiles and homes. Observes Lendol Calder in his book, *Financing the American Dream,*

> Without credit financing, the automobile would not so quickly have reached, and perhaps never have reached, a true mass market, and its impact on American life would have taken a very different course. . . . From the standpoint of car buyers, the greatest watershed event in the history of the automobile was . . . the discovery that automobiles could be bought on the installment plan.[4]

Such loans were anathema to bankers, who were used to making loans to businesses and farmers, where the collateral was a productive and profit-making asset. As a result, auto companies stepped in to offer credit themselves.

The finance subsidiary of General Motors, the General Motors Acceptance Corporation, opened its doors in March 1919. By 1924, nearly 75% of cars were bought on credit. From there, the idea spread to all sorts of other consumer durables. "By 1930, installment credit financed the sales of 60–75% of automobiles, 80–90% of furniture, 75% of washing machines, 65% of vacuum cleaners, 18–25% of jewelry, 75% of radio sets, and 80% of phonographs."[5]

Consumer installment loans almost tripled from 1919 to

1929. Indeed, consumers took on almost $1 billion in consumer debt in 1929 alone, an enormous amount in a $100 billion economy.[6] And consumer credit indirectly helped finance the stock market boom as well, since the market leaders were the auto companies and such highfliers as RCA—major beneficiaries of the rise of consumer credit.

On top of that, there was an explosion of mortgage debt that made the boom even bigger. Altogether, individual and noncorporate debt increased by $29 billion in the decade ending in 1929, but disposable personal income increased by only $20 billion.

THE DARK SIDE OF FINANCIAL INNOVATION

Creating new forms of finance is like a wizard calling up a powerful spirit. Access to new capital opens up the door to powerful booms, as the power of the financial markets are extended to broader areas of the economy. But the cost of that power has greater potential for destruction.

In the second half of the 1800s, for example, the creation of national stock and bond markets made possible large-scale investment in railroads and other capital-intensive industries. But the new capital markets also opened the door to national financial panics as well as investment booms and busts on a national scale. Businesses were no longer subject only to local economic conditions, but were tied, via the credit markets, to events across the country and even the globe.

Wesley Clair Mitchell, one of the preeminent economists of the early 20th century and the founding director of the National Bureau of Economic Research, wrote in his 1913 classic *Business Cycles:*

> As handicraft gave place to factories managed on business principles, catering to a wide and uncertain market, entering

freely into long-term contracts, requiring a heavy investment of fixed capital, and using borrowed money on a liberal scale, the circle of enterprise affected by financial difficulties grew steadily larger, and the danger that financial difficulties would arise from the conduct of business affairs grew steadily greater.[7]

The business cycle continued to evolve in the early 20th century, as the invention of consumer credit brought the power of the financial markets into the home. Booms became bigger and longer, since now not just businesses but consumers as well could spend substantially in excess of their resources.

But the busts became deeper and more pervasive as well. In the aftermath of the 1929 crash, debt-laden consumers pulled back on spending. Some economic historians have suggested that this plunge in consumer spending was at least as important a cause of the economic slowdown in 1930 as any drop-off in business investment.[8] Indeed, it was more than just a response to layoffs and falling stock prices. Overextended American consumers took the stock market crash as a signal to hunker down, beyond what a rational assessment of lost wealth and income would have predicted.

MISPLACED CONFIDENCE

The run-up in consumer borrowing in the 1920s came against a backdrop of pervasive confidence in both the strength of the U.S. economy and the potency of the Federal Reserve. Americans believed that they had a new and better approach to organizing business, which was inevitably going to supplant the old ways. As one historian wrote of the 1920s:

> A doctrine began to emerge which held that the U.S. had both an opportunity and an obligation to chart a fresh and

uniquely American course towards human betterment. . . .
The United States had a mission to serve humanity by demon-
strating the superiority of a distinctive 'American way.'[9]

It wasn't just Americans who believed in the superiority of the
U.S. system. Europeans, too, saw the American success and
wanted to know how it was done. In 1926, two young British engineers, Bertram Austin and W. Francis Lloyd, came back from a
visit to the U.S. and wrote a book entitled *The Secret of High Wages*
that attempted to describe, for a European audience, the principles behind the American prosperity. Walter T. Layton, then
editor of *The Economist,* wrote an introduction to the book:

> No European can visit America without realizing that across
> the Atlantic changes are occurring which amount to an eco-
> nomic revolution. Tens of millions of people have attained
> there standards of comfort and of culture far higher than
> those of any other country in the world to-day, and immensely
> in excess of anything hitherto known in the world's history;
> while the rate of material advancement has accelerated to
> breakneck speed.[10]

Here are some of the principles Austin and Lloyd identified
as key to the U.S. success story:[11]

> "It is more advantageous to increase total profits by reducing
> prices to the consumer."
> "The productive capacity *per capita* of labor can be increased
> without limit depending upon the progress made in time and
> trouble-saving appliances."
> "It is better that labor should be rewarded by wages bearing
> some relation to output rather than by a fixed wage."
> "Research and experimental work are of prime importance to
> progress."

Oddly enough, all of these principles from the 1920s would
seem quite familiar in the 1990s as well. And, as in the 1990s, the

powerful belief that the U.S. had uncovered the key to permanent economic success was reflected in the exuberance of Americans. They took on debt and made risky investments as if their prosperity were unbounded.

THE RISE OF THE FEDERAL RESERVE

The other pillar of Americans' self-confidence in the 1920s was their trust in the Federal Reserve's ability to smooth out the economy's ups and downs. The Fed was created in 1913 after a series of financial crises—including the failure of a major Wall Street bank in 1907—produced bipartisan support for a strong central bank that could control the new industrial economy and keep the credit flowing. Democrats favored a strong central bank as a way of stopping the so-called Wall Street money trust from cutting off credit to farmers during financial crises. If the money supply was under government control, they felt, the number and severity of credit crunches would be reduced. The Wall Street banks, meanwhile, eventually accepted the fact that a strong Fed was a necessary protection against financial panics.

The new Federal Reserve System, comprised of a central bank and twelve regional banks, enjoyed growing support as American businessmen and investors felt someone was finally in charge of the economy. "The System took—and perhaps even more was given—credit for the generally stable conditions that prevailed, and high hopes were placed in the potency of monetary policy,"[12] wrote Milton Friedman. "Bankers and businessmen . . . regarded its powers with awe."[13]

This period marked the early stages of modern macroeconomic management, as the Fed began to learn how to use its powers of monetary control to stabilize the economy. For example, it raised rates in 1923 to cut off an impending inventory boom. There was a general feeling that under the auspices of a watchful Fed eye, "relatively stable prices and the avoidance of speculative inventory accumulations would ensure permanent prosperity."[14]

The economic ups and downs that remained were no longer so worrisome. "We seem to have made some considerable progress toward correcting the swings of the rhythm and toward smoothing out the fluctuations in activity which are its worst social manifestations," wrote Rex Tugwell in a 1927 book. Tugwell, a Columbia University economist who later went on to play a crucial role in the New Deal, added:

> Our present control of currency is apparently, if we may judge by the experience of the past few years, achieving a stability which is entirely unprecedented. . . . If this stability can be maintained, one of the worst features of the cycle will have been obviated[15].

No longer an unpredictable animal, the economy came to be seen as a machine with regular movements that could be fine-tuned. The oscillations of the business cycle were no longer crises that threatened to destroy the economy, but "the 'heart-throb' of a lively, dynamic system."[16] Dips in the stock market or the economy would be followed by predictable rises. Investment, consumption, and prices all moved together in a way that could be anticipated and predicted. The business cycle became a source of comfort, not fear.

OVER THE CLIFF

But this feeling of comfort and confidence was misplaced. When the boom ended, what followed was not just a tame and controlled downturn, as most had expected, but a massive depression. There is still disagreement among economists about whether the October 1929 stock market crash constituted an inevitable reaction to a speculative bubble, a response to international financial turmoil, or the unintended consequence of Fed tightening. At the time, though, it came as a surprise to almost everyone.

The Depression hit every sector of the economy—agriculture, construction, foreign trade—but the greatest pain, by far, was inflicted on the heart of the industrial economy. As we will see in Chapter 5, the industries that led the boom—the automobile industry and its suppliers—started to fall in the spring of 1929, well before the rest of the economy turned down. What's more, these core manufacturing industries, which had transformed the economy and the lives of Americans, absorbed the brunt of the destruction as the early stages of the Depression unfolded.

The depths of the collapse were staggering. In the twelve months prior to October 1929, America's automobile factories produced over 4.7 million cars. In the year after the crash, automobile production fell by 40%, as consumers simply stopped buying. By 1932, production had fallen to only 1.1 million cars, 75% below its peak. Over the stretch from 1929 to 1932, the number of automobile production workers fell by 45%, a decline that traumatized whole states. And that drop underestimates the economic impact: auto company payroll expenses actually dropped by 65%.

Or consider machine tools. These were the sinews of the industrial age, providing the machinery that made factories go. But that put them right in the path of the Depression. From 1929 to 1932 the machine tool industry laid off or fired 60% of its workers, many of them highly skilled.

Business and labor were stuck in a vicious circle. Companies laid off workers to save money, which removed buying power from the economy, which led to more cutbacks. The electric power industry as a whole ran a profit every year through the Depression, but did so by cutting back capital spending and maintenance expenditures from $1 billion in 1930 to $200 million in 1933.[17]

As a result, the number of workers with jobs in electrical equipment factories also dropped by about 60%.

Even the good news was bad news. Despite the Depression, manufacturing productivity rose by almost 10% between 1929 and 1933, due to better production techniques and improvements in factory equipment. But that meant even fewer workers were needed to make a diminishing amount of products.

With astonishing virulence, the disaster spread across the entire country. In New York State, the first year of the Depression saw a 27% drop in the number employed in the textile industry, and an 18% drop in apparel jobs. Payrolls plummeted even farther. In Texas, employment in foundries and machine shops dropped by almost 40%.[18] And the nightmare just kept getting worse and worse. State and local governments, running out of money, were forced to cut spending and hiring just as everything turned bad. "When local taxes fell 20 or 30 percent behind payment, cities cut their costs by reducing such services as maintaining roads and clearing snow."[19] Construction spending by state and local governments fell by about 20% in 1931, which put even more laborers and others out of work.[20] School budgets were chopped by 26% between 1930 and 1934. That meant shorter hours for schools and, in some cases, forced closings.

The financial system simply seemed to implode. The Standard and Poor's stock average fell from a high of about 32 in 1929 to less than 5 in 1932. The sheer duration of the bad years contributed to the despair. People ran through their savings and lost their homes and farms. About a third of national banks went out of business. "To a middle class that had been raised on the virtues of thrift," wrote one historian, "nothing was more devastating than a bank failure."[21]

The feeling that no one was in charge of the economy helped fuel a rising tide of political turmoil and violence. American Federation of Labor president William Green said in 1931: "When despite every effort to get employment, men and women find no opportunity to earn their living, desperation and blind revolt follow."[22] In the summer of 1932, twenty-five thousand destitute war veterans marched on Washington, asking for prepayment of bonuses not actually due them until 1945. Also in 1932, police fired on three thousand demonstrators marching on Ford's River Rouge plant, killing four of them. It seemed like only a matter of time before the whole country would erupt in violence.

The Depression spread across the entire globe. Financial panics ricocheted from one country to the next, and in a misguided effort to keep money and gold from flowing out, central banks in virtually every country raised interest rates, making the situation far worse. Almost every major stock market fell by at least 50%, and most did not recover for decades. The annual volume of world trade collapsed from $3 billion in 1929 to less than $1 billion in 1933. And not to be ignored are the political consequences: the spreading global turmoil contributed mightily to the ascent of the Nazi Party to power in Germany, setting the stage for World War II.

FEARS OF A REPEAT

A combination of the New Deal, looser monetary policy, and World War II finally pulled the U.S. out of depression. Yet having once plunged into a hidden crevasse, Americans were wary of the next one. After World War II ended, economists worried that the country would fall back into another depression when the nation demobilized and the impetus of military spending was gone.

That didn't happen, but the fear didn't go away. It came back again in the 1970s, when runaway inflation, soaring unemployment, and gas rationing made the U.S. economy feel as if it were out of control. In 1982, when the unemployment rate went over 10% for the first time since the 1930s, there was public hand-wringing about an impending depression. In 1986, Edward S. Hyman Jr., a respected Wall Street economist, was quoted in *Business Week* as saying that the odds were 3 in 10 that "the course we're on will lead to a depression sometime between 1990 and 1995."[23] And when the 1987 stock market crash sent the U.S. market plunging down by 23% in a single day—a far bigger single-day decline in percentage terms than the crash of 1929—no one could avoid worrying whether depression would follow this time as well.

Even after the economy sailed through the 1987 crash apparently unscathed, the fears did not disappear completely. During the recession of 1990–91, the looming danger was the failure of major commercial banks. Citibank, the world's largest bank, was apparently teetering on the edge of insolvency, raising the prospect of a cascading run of bank failures that could overwhelm the deposit insurance system put in place after the Great Depression. In 1990, the head of the General Accounting Office testified before the Senate that "not since its birth during the Great Depression has the federal system of deposit insurance for commercial banks faced such a period of danger and uncertainty as it does today."

COULD IT HAPPEN AGAIN?

The government clearly has the policy tools to sustain demand and employment, if it will use them. Monetary stimulus, and to a lesser extent, fiscal stimulus, have proven to be quite effective in boosting demand and keeping financial markets afloat. In addition, time and again Federal Reserve Chairman Alan Greenspan has shown himself to be extremely adroit at steering the economy through rough terrain.

But the mostly successful management of recessions and expansions in recent years has given rise to a false sense of security. The U.S. is no longer a country of factories, where the key objective is to keep the assembly lines humming at full speed and Americans fully employed, without letting inflation spiral out of control.

Instead, the microprocessor and the Internet rule, and policymakers face a very different problem: how to maintain the flow of innovations and productivity gains that are driving the New Economy forward. These goals will require a new approach to managing the economy, one that takes into account the links between technological change and the financial markets. If such a vision is not forthcoming, there could be enormous damage to the economy and to the welfare of Americans.

CHAPTER FOUR

The Tech Cycle

ECONOMISTS LIKE to say that "there ain't no such thing as a free lunch." The expression, popularized by University of Chicago economist Milton Friedman but dating back to at least 1949, is shorthand for saying that nothing comes without a price.[1] It's a basic principle that applies to almost any situation.

To some, it looks like the New Economy has repealed the law of "no free lunch." People seem to get rich with only a few years of hard work. Hotmail, Yahoo, and others provide free e-mail. And the economy seems to grow faster with less volatility and less inflation. In his recent book, *The Wealth of Choices,* Alan Murray, head of the *Wall Street Journal's* Washington bureau, writes: "In the New Economy, recessions seem less likely."[2]

But the smiley-face version of the New Economy has always been more myth than reality. The trade-offs have not disappeared, only shifted. Many people who went to dot.coms worked incredibly hard and saw their stock options end up being worth nothing when the Internet stocks crashed in early 2000. Free e-mail service comes with ads built in, and often slower service.

Perhaps most important, rather than having been repealed, the business cycle has been reincarnated in a different garb for the information age. The tech cycle is characterized by long, extended booms followed by deep downturns that can conceivably go on for years. Most of us know what a tech boom looks like—we've all lived through one. But at this writing, none of us have lived through a tech bust. To know what *that* looks like, we first have to understand something about the tech cycle and how it works. That's what this chapter is about.

On the upward swing of the tech cycle, growth is rapid, unemployment is low, and business investment is strong. Moreover, inflation is dormant even when growth is strong, since new technology drives up productivity and opens the door for new competitors. The stock market soars, fueling risk capital for new companies and faster innovation. This cycle feeds on itself.

But that strength is also the New Economy's weakness. When the virtuous circle finally goes in reverse, all the factors that sustained the economy will head in the other direction. The rate of technological change, the rate of productivity improvements, and the level of business investment will all fall. Inflation will accelerate, and the stock market will tank. To top it off, when the stock market sags, there won't be such a big payoff from IPOs of startups. The flow of venture capital into new businesses will fall off, and the pace of innovation will slow even further. Just as widespread layoffs in the Old Economy reduced consumer demand for manufactured goods, causing further layoffs, the New Economy has its own vicious cycle: a technological slowdown leads to a depressed stock market, which leads to further technological slowdown (see Table 4.1).

In the New Economy, the prominent role of risk capital creates the opportunity for new kinds of economic swings, rather than an exemption from recessions. Innovation booms can and will be followed by innovation slumps, recessions, or even depressions.

TECHNOLOGY AND THE BUSINESS CYCLE

The U.S. entered the 1990s with economists in rare agreement about the causes and nature of recessions. The story went

Table 4.1   The Tech Cycle

Expansion Phase	Contraction Phase
Rapid introduction of new technology and new business models	Technological stagnation
Easy availability of funding for new and innovative businesses; easy for new competitors to enter	Little funding available for risky startups; difficult for new competitors to emerge
Strong productivity growth	Weak productivity growth
Investment booms, as companies try to keep up with new technology	Investment falls sharply
Inflation is held down by productivity gains, competitive pressures for new firms, and rapidly declining prices of new technology	Inflation rebounds, as productivity slows, new startups become less common, and the price of new technology doesn't fall as quickly.
Buoyant stock markets	Depressed stock markets

something like this. Over the course of an expansion, the economy overheats, unemployment falls too low, wages start heading up, and inflation surges. In response, the Federal Reserve raises interest rates, putting the brakes on interest rate–sensitive sectors such as housing, automobiles, and business investment. The resulting recession pushes up unemployment and drives down inflation. Then the whole process starts over again.

This story makes no explicit mention of technology. But look under the hood of any macroeconomic forecasting model, and you'll see that technological change is implicitly assumed to be a *stabilizing* force. Even during recession years, when jobs, inflation, and GDP are plunging, the underlying technological capabilities of the economy are assumed to increase at a constant pace.

The assumption is that a steady stream of inventions, innovations, and new products comes out of universities, government laboratories, and corporate R&D operations no matter what is happening in the rest of the economy. These are not necessarily big breakthroughs. They could be little tweaks that improve the efficiency of a factory, the carrying capacity of a telecommunications network, or the ease of making an airplane reservation. This flow of innovations, combined with capital investment, steadily improves the productivity of workers, and gives the economy a natural bias toward growth. In today's macroeconomic models, the underlying growth rate of labor productivity is about 3% or so per year. That moderates any recession, at least according to the models, and makes it difficult to have a steep economic decline.[3]

Think of the economy as a ski lift chair being pulled up a mountainside on a cable attached to a motor. The chair can bounce around and sway in the wind, and the passengers may even feel a bit queasy. Nevertheless, the chair will keep rising up the mountain as long as the motor keeps turning.

Even in the conventional view, the technology motor may break down over time. Starving the education system of money will eventually mean that there are not enough skilled workers. Cutbacks in R&D spending will eventually show up as a slower rate of innovation. And sometimes the motor just slows of its own accord, as it seemed to do in the 1970s. But generally these problems are assumed to develop only slowly, and are not thought to have a big impact on the short-term ups and downs of the economy.

TECHNOLOGY AS A DESTABILIZING INFLUENCE

In the Old Economy, this assumption of a steady flow of innovations was not necessarily wrong. Obviously, funding of government and university research doesn't vary all much with the business cycle. And studies have shown that for big companies, there is little relationship between company cash flow and R&D outlays.[4]

But the New Economy has changed the dynamics of innovation. In key leading-edge industries, such as information technology and biotechnology, more and more innovation is done by small companies, funded by profit-minded venture capitalists with an eye toward making a big killing. In other words, innovation is becoming *disintermediated*—moved out of big organizations into the marketplace.

Over the long run, this is an extremely positive development. As we saw in Chapter 2, the availability of risk capital greatly accelerates the rate at which new firms bring innovations to market, and the rate at which they are adopted by existing businesses.

But the shift to risk-capital funding means that the innovative impulse is no longer immune from recessions. When the economy and the stock market slide, so does the funding for innovative new businesses—and not by any small amount. In the aftermath of the 1987 crash, venture capital fell by more than 50%, from $5.2 billion in 1987 to $2.6 billion in 1991. The availability of venture capital rises and falls with the Nasdaq stock market index, although with wider swings (Figure 4.1).

A 50% fall today would send investment funding plunging from roughly $50 billion in 1999 to $25 billion or less. That sounds like levels of investment would still be high, but remember that the information technology sector is far bigger, and far more important to the economy, than it was just a few years ago. At that new level, fewer companies would be funded, for lower amounts. Venture capitalists would aim for safer bets.

So in the New Economy, any stock market or economic slowdown is likely to be accompanied by a slowdown in innovation. With less funding available and fewer companies started, there will be less of an impetus to get new applications and ideas to market. What's more, with a less formidable threat from well-funded startups, existing companies will be under less pressure to quickly adopt new innovations that might require painful restructuring. The result is a slowdown in underlying productivity growth.

The key point is that the role of innovation in the economy has changed. Where it once was a steadying influence, damping

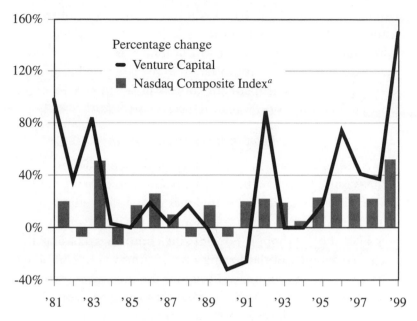

Figure 4.1   Venture Capital and the Stock Market
Source: National Venture Capital Association.
[a]Annual average.

the swings in the business cycle, it now accentuates them. Rather than moderating the next recession, innovation will make it worse. Rather than providing a floor for the economy, technological change—or the sudden lack of it—will open a trapdoor. Here's what will happen as innovation slows.

Slowdown in Productivity Growth

There are many new products and innovations still in the pipeline. Nevertheless, as the underlying rate of technological change slows, productivity growth will slow as well. There will be fewer breakthroughs such as the web browser to spur investment and change, and the rate at which existing firms adopt innovations will slow as well.

A lower rate of productivity growth will show up as a slower GDP growth rate. For example, a 1% increase in hours worked combined with a 3% increase in output per hour (productivity) leads to a 4% increase in GDP—but if productivity growth is lower, the increase in output will be lower as well. Moreover, there will be a tendency for inflation to rise since in the absence of big productivity gains, companies will be forced to boost prices if their wage or raw material costs rise.

Slowdown in Investment Growth

As we saw in Chapter 2, much of the investment boom of the 1990s was predicated on the rapid introduction of new products and services, which forced companies to keep investing simply to keep up with competitors. This was the racehorse effect, or if you like, the greyhound effect (with companies chasing the high-tech rabbit). But a slowing rate of innovation, combined with a weakening economy, will reduce the incentives to invest.

Existing corporations will have less reason to spend good dollars on speculative investments, such as web sites that don't earn any revenue. And they will have less reason to quickly adopt risky new innovations, because their competition won't be doing it. For example, rather than upgrade their computers every two years, companies will choose to wait a little longer. But even a shift from a two-year upgrade cycle to a three-year cycle—on the face of it not much of a change—would effectively cut a company's annual computer purchases by one third.

The Return of Inflation

On the downward swing of the tech cycle, the economy will paradoxically become much more inflation-prone. When productivity growth slows and investment falls off, it will become harder for companies to absorb wage increases without raising prices. And large companies will have less reason to restrain themselves because they will have less fear of competition from startups. That suggests the downturn is likely to see an increase in the pricing power of large firms, especially in the early years of the decline.

Moreover, the slowing of innovation will have a direct effect on inflation. In the second half of the 1990s, rapidly falling prices for software and information technology equipment sliced about a half percentage point off the inflation rate (as measured by the GDP deflator). As the rate of innovation slows, it's likely that tech prices will fall at a slower rate. That could add significantly to inflation all by itself.

The Collapse of the Stock Market

When the tech cycle turns down, all of the positive factors that sustained the stock market in the late 1990s will reverse. Venture capital falls, and the number of IPOs shrinks. The flow of innovations tapers off, productivity growth slows, and profits get squeezed. Companies start raising prices, and inflation accelerates. The combined effect on the stock market will be nothing less than toxic.

This is not a small matter. In an Old Economy recession, profits fall—which is bad for equities—but so do inflation and interest rates, which has the effect of buoying up stocks. Thus the stock market traditionally did not move together with the rest of the economy, which muted the business cycle to some degree. In fact, depending on what variables you look at, there can actually be a small *negative* correlation between movements in the stock market and changes in income. For example, in the years in which the increase in disposable income is small, the market value of stocks actually tends to increase more than average[5].

But in the New Economy, the stock market is synchronized with the swings of the tech cycle, creating the potential for much steeper downturns than before.

THE COMING VENTURE BUST

In some ways, it seems as if venture capital shouldn't be affected that much by a bear market or an economic downturn. Exciting new technologies, such as superconductors or biotech or the Internet, create new opportunities for long-term investments with the potential for big returns in the future, no matter what else is happening in the economy. Indeed, investors in venture funds put the money in for ten years or more, and venture capitalists will proclaim "we are in this for the long haul."

But almost by definition successful venture capitalists have finely tuned antennae for the profitability of their investments. The willingness to invest in a new firm depends on the expected future return. And getting a good return requires a strong stock market, because the most profitable exit strategy by far is to take the startup public. Thus the supply of venture capital funds to entrepreneurs is closely linked to the stock market.[6]

In fact, risk capital is much more sensitive to the state of the economy and the stock market than are most other forms of credit. Venture capital and IPOs are very high-risk investments, and those are exactly the sort of financial markets that you would expect to close down when things get bumpy. Notes economist F. M. Scherer, "Partly, because investors often respond to evidence of strong past performance rather than unbiased estimates of future performance, there are pronounced cycles in venture investment levels."[7]

At the top of the tech cycle, exuberant venture capitalists provide buckets of money to seemingly anyone who asks (although even then there is a lot of picking and choosing). The possibilities of the technology of the day seem limitless—whether it is biotechnology, superconductors, or e-commerce. Existing firms appear flabby, slow, and ripe to be plucked. And investors are ready to walk over their mother (okay, maybe their brother) to get a piece of a hot IPO. For example, when Netscape went public in August 1995, the S&P index was up by about 20% over the previous year. That helped lift Netscape's stock offering.

If the market had been down by 20% instead, it would have been a lot harder for Netscape to raise money. In a weak or unsettled stock market even a technologically viable project will have much more difficulty attracting sufficient financing. Moreover, the weakness in the markets hurts financing for startups in all industries, since they are all linked through the financial markets. At the bottom of the tech cycle, when fewer businesses of all types get funded, the pendulum swings away from the riskier, more innovative bets to "safer" companies with proven track records.

In fact, it's easy to find startups that failed, in part, because they needed money and financing at a time when the venture and IPO markets were closed. Part of the demise of the Osborne Computer Corporation, for example, was simply bad timing. Founded in 1980 by entrepreneur Adam Osborne, the company introduced the first portable personal computer for the mass market in 1981. By the fall of 1982, the company's sole product, the Osborne I computer, was selling well.

A year later the company filed for bankruptcy. What happened? Although they had made their share of mistakes, one of their biggest problems was that they could not get sufficient financing to get their new products out the door quickly enough to compete with IBM. Because the stock market languished through most of the recession year of 1982, it was extremely difficult for any company to go public. There were only thirty-nine venture-backed IPOs in 1982 (compared to 196 the next year), raising a minuscule $576 million. So Osborne had to delay its IPO—and by the time the financing window opened again, it was too late to catch up with IBM.

Venture financing ebbed away again in the aftermath of the 1987 crash. Between 1987 and 1991, first-round financing for new companies—that is, companies that had never gotten venture capital before—fell by 75% (see Table 4.2).

Even the most experienced venture capitalists grow more cautious when financial conditions turn tight. In 1990, for example, Tim Draper, a leading venture capitalist, told one magazine that

Table 4.2   The Last Downturn in Venture Capital

	Peak (year)	Trough (year)	Percentage Decline
Venture capital disbursements (billions of dollars)	$5.19 (1988)	$2.57 (1991)	–51
First-round funding (billions of dollars)	$2.44 (1988)	$0.61 (1991)	–75
Number of companies receiving first-round funding	723 (1987)	283 (1991)	–61
Commitments to venture capital funds by investors (billions of dollars)	$5.45 (1989)	$1.49 (1991)	–73

Source: National Venture Capital Association.

venture capitalists are "not going to fund a couple of people coming out of Stanford as easily as they would have in 1983. Instead, they're going to wait until these people have succeeded for a while."[8]

Exuberance turns to caution and then pessimism. By 1991, for example, as venture funding continued to fall, there was a growing sense that venture capital had lost its nerve. As Michael Schrage wrote in the *Los Angeles Times,*

> Where venture capital once was a high-octane fuel driving the creation and commercialization of new technologies, it is now more like a lawn sprinkler under water rationing. . . . By and large, venture capital is likely to be less of a positive force in this decade than it was in the last.[9]

Around the same time, another article appeared in the *Los Angeles Times* with the title "Dream of Striking It Rich Fading in Silicon Valley":

> It is now clear to all but the most blindly ambitious that the vision of entrepreneurial riches is mostly myth. . . . Today, most

observers agree, a company such as Apple would probably never get off the ground. Venture capitalists would be unlikely to fund the likes of Steve Jobs and Steve Wozniak, who were barely out of their teens and had no business experience when they founded Apple.[10]

The inability to raise money from venture capital or the stock market forces startups, even those with good technologies, to seek alliances and funding from large domestic and foreign corporations with deep pockets. But these substitutes, on balance, give worse outcomes, presumably because the larger company distorts the decisions of the startups. For example, a recent study of small biotech firms showed that those that were forced to turn to large companies for funding were not as innovative. The authors of the study, Josh Lerner and Alexander Tsai, note, "contracts that are signed at times when biotechnology firms are raising little external financing and that assign the most control rights to the large corporation perform significantly worse."[11]

Attempts by foreign corporations to buy up American innovative companies seem to run into the same problem. In the late 1980s—a slow period for venture capital and IPOs—small high-tech startups turned to large Japanese companies for money. At the time, many felt that this reflected flaws in the U.S. economic model, and foretold a future when the U.S. economy would lose its technological edge.

But in fact much of the problem had to do with the lack of venture capital for small firms in the U.S. and the buoyant Japanese stock market. The combination meant that the main source of money for startups was overseas.

Yet most Japanese purchases of U.S. technology did not pay off. For example, when Andrew Heller, a highly regarded computer designer from IBM, founded Hal Computer Systems in 1990, he couldn't get enough financing from venture capitalists and had to sell a substantial portion of the company to Fujitsu to raise money. The business didn't die, but it never really took off and was eventually folded into Fujitsu completely. The same thing happened to Poqet Computer, which in early 1990 started shipping the Poqet PC, the first pocket-sized MS-DOS-compatible computer. Because of the paucity of venture funding, it too had to sell a big chunk of itself to Fujitsu. Once again, the business ended up languishing.

The inescapable conclusion is that, at least for now, there really is no good substitute for venture capital when the market turns down. When the virtuous cycle of innovation and profit turns vicious, there is no obvious counterbalancing mechanism to stop the slowdown.

HIGH-TECH, HIGH VOLATILITY

There is an additional factor that further aggravates the downswing of the tech cycle. It turns out that the very nature of high-tech industries makes them much more prone to boom-and-bust cycles. Their heavy investments in R&D and new capital equipment are a godsend when the economy is strong, but when growth turns down, they have a lot of expenses that they cannot cut without eviscerating the future.

Compared to most other parts of the economy, high-tech firms are future-oriented. They have to invest heavily in new product development and new equipment in order to keep up with competitors and with the pace of technological change. Intel has two or three generations of microprocessors in development at once; Microsoft programmers are writing and debugging code for the next generation of Windows. Telecom firms spend tens of billions of dollars each year building new infrastructure in the expectation of generating profits in the future.

New Economy companies spend far more, relative to their size, on research and development and capital expenditures than do other companies. The top software, hardware, telecom, and Internet companies devote 30%, 40%, and even 50% of their budgets to future-oriented activities (Table 4.3). For example, Microsoft spent about $3 billion on R&D in fiscal year 1999, compared to only $10 billion or so on all operating expenses. Intel spent almost $7 billion on R&D and capital spending combined, compared to roughly $19 billion in operating expenses. In 1999, total capital spending by the largest telephone companies totaled over $60 billion.

By comparison, the average R&D and capital spending by an S&P 500 firm was much lower, roughly 12% of operating expenses.[12] Many Old Economy companies devoted as little as 5% or less of their resources to these future-oriented activities.

The high-tech firms' large investments are all justified on the

Table 4.3   Betting on the Future

Capital expenditures and R&D spending as share of operating expenses.[a]

eBay	50%
Webvan	47%
RealNetworks	47%
U S West	40%[b]
Advanced Micro Devices	40%
Pfizer	37%
Microsoft	36%
Texas Instruments	35%
Intel	35%
Bell Atlantic	35%[b]
Eli Lilly	34%
BellSouth	33%[b]
Cisco	29%
Average for all S&P 500 companies reporting both capital expenditures and R&D spending	12%

Source: Standard & Poor's Compustat.

[a]Operating expenses defined as operating revenue minus operating income. Based on most current fiscal year data available as of mid-May 2000.

[b]Capital spending only.

basis of expected growth in the economy and markets. They are placing tremendous bets on the future. If growth slows for long enough, it will turn out that these high-tech companies have invested too much too fast, and must start cutting back their R&D and capital investments. And a large number of high-tech workers will find themselves on the street.

Here's another way to look at the same thing. Many high-tech industries exhibit increasing returns to scale. This means that as companies get larger, their average cost of production, per unit of output, tends to fall. For example, if it costs $10 million to write and debug a new program, and $1 to make each additional copy on a CD-ROM, then the average cost of the first copy of the program is just over $10 million. The average cost of the tenth copy is just over $1 million. But the time you have produced 10 million copies, the average cost has fallen to $2 per copy.

Increasing returns to scale have often been cited as one of the big advantages of the information age. For example, Kevin Kelly, in his book, *New Rules for the New Economy,* writes: "In the industrial economy success was self-limiting; it obeyed the law of decreasing returns. In the network economy, success is self-reinforcing; it obeys the law of increasing returns."[13]

But what people fail to realize is that increasing-returns-to-scale firms, like tropical orchids, thrive best in hothouse conditions. The faster they can expand, the more economies of scale they generate and the bigger profits they make. In a fast-growth environment, it makes sense to incur high upfront costs and expect to recoup them as existing markets grow and new ones open up.

A growing economy is even more essential for dot.coms. Their task is far easier if they can take a slice of a growing market, rather than having to take sales away from existing brick-and-mortar retailers in a stagnant market.

But when growth slows or goes in reverse, firms still have large fixed costs, without as much revenue to cover them. A recession makes increasing-returns-to-scale firms less efficient and less profitable quickly. They don't have the option of cutting their orders for raw materials or laying off production workers—they have relatively little of both. Their only recourse is to mortgage their future by slowing the development of new products.

That's quite clear in the case of telecom networks. The telecom companies are investing in increased bandwidth capacity under the assumption that demand will grow fast enough to justify the heavy cost. But if for some reason demand falls significantly short of forecasts, the telecoms have no way to get the money they spent back.

To be sure, the wealthiest New Economy companies can keep investing even when times turn bad. Cash-rich Intel Corp. increased capital spending by 60% in 1990 and by another 40% in 1991, despite the recession. Such a strategy, if adopted by enough businesses, would help smooth out small business fluctuations and prolong the expansion.

But for most New Economy companies, if the demand really falls short of expectations, there may simply be no way to cover costs without cutting back sharply on future-oriented expenses: R&D and capital investment. And once that happens, it is the kiss of death.

Moreover, these cutbacks will put further downward pressure on the rest of the economy, and make the tech downswing worse. It's worth noting that in the late 1980s, several economists published research papers suggesting that economies with increasing returns to scale tended to be much less stable. As one author put it, increasing returns to scale "amplify the economy's response to shocks arising from any source."[14] In lay terms, that means you can have big swings in the economy from very small shocks.

At the time, this research was basically dismissed as irrelevant because most economists believed that increasing-returns-to-scale industries were relatively rare in the U.S. economy. But high-tech is taking up a larger and larger portion of the economy. It may turn out that the real world has finally caught up with theory. The same increasing-returns-to-scale industries that led the last expansion of the 20th century may also lead the first downturn of the 21st.

CHAPTER FIVE

The Long, Slow Slide

WHILE THE SUN is shining, it's hard to prepare for rain. Similarly, while the U.S. economy is in the midst of the longest expansion on record, it's difficult to imagine that the prosperity is ever going to come to an end.

But let us look beyond the tech boom to the dark side of the New Economy. The downturn is likely to come, as violent and destructive as a hurricane. For investors, workers, and managers trying to prepare for the tech downturn, there are three key questions.

First: What are the indications that the economy has peaked and the good times will soon be over? These are difficult to read, but history suggests some signs to look for in advance of a downturn.

Second: What industries and occupations will get hit by the New Economy bust? The downside of the tech cycle will not be centered in the automobile and steel factories, which were the leading edge of the downturn of the 1930s. It will hit hardest at the new information technology and communications industries that drove growth in the 1990s.

Finally, the most important question of all: How long will the downturn last—and will it turn into a depression? After nearly a decade of prosperity, most households and businesses have built up enough of a cushion to ride out a short downturn, no matter how scary it feels at the time, and focus on the long run. But the same forces that drove the lengthy boom can make the tech downturn deeper and longer than expected. And if policymakers let the bad times go on too long, the appropriate strategy changes. Everyone starts to hunker down for the long run: smart investors shift from equities to less risky investments, households pull back on spending, workers choose safe jobs, businesses cut capital investment and hiring. Once that happens, the economy gets locked into a slow growth path—in other words, a depression for the Internet age. Because the Internet Depression will be so different from anything we have seen in the past, the safeguards put in place in the 1930s to prevent a repeat of the Great Depression will no longer be sufficient. Depression could become the norm—and that would be the biggest disaster of all.

DISTRESS SIGNALS

A powerful economy like that of the U.S. does not break in a week, a few months, or even a year. It possesses enormous reserves of vitality and wealth that carry it through setbacks. As a result, the shift from tech boom to tech bust will be a lengthy process. It could take up to two years from the peak of the stock market to the moment when the economy conclusively falls into depression.

Moreover, at each step along the way, the data will be misleading, noisy, and difficult to sort out. Confusion will be inevitable, since the downside of the tech cycle is uncharted territory. Many people will be sure that the slowdown is only a pause and that the economy and Wall Street are sure to come roaring back.

Nevertheless, there will be certain critical early signs that the New Economy is losing altitude (see Table 5.1). The clearest and most important is the behavior of the stock market, particularly

Table 5.1   Early Signs of the End of the Tech Boom

- Simultaneous fall in tech stocks and slowdown in tech spending
- Slowdown in the rate of price declines for tech goods
- Decline in the flow of venture capital and initial public offerings

the tech sector, assessed in combination with data on corporate spending on information technology. When both tech spending and tech stocks turn down simultaneously, that's a strong sign that the New Economy boom may be nearing the end.

In the Old Economy, the stock market was at best a mediocre predictor of the performance of the economy. The reason was simple: during good times, both profits and inflation rose, and during tough times, both profits and inflation fell. Since profits are a plus for stocks and inflation is a minus, these two forces tended to push equity prices in opposite directions. As a result, the market did not move consistently with the economy at all. As Nobel laureate economist Paul Samuelson once joked, the stock market "has accurately predicted nine of the past five recessions."

The 1987 crash is a good example of a market event with no apparent effect on the real economy. Economic growth for the two years after the 1987 crash was 3.9%, considerably faster than the 3.2% rate in the two years before. Similarly, a flat stock market from 1976 to 1979 did not stop the economy from growing at a 4.4% pace.

But in the New Economy, the stock market, especially the tech-heavy Nasdaq, has a much more intimate relationship with the growth of the real economy. A fall in the market directly affects the amount of risk capital available for new startups, which reduces the rate of technological innovation and productivity growth. That in turn feeds back into the stock market, which goes down as productivity and profit growth slow, and inflation rises— all of which are negative for equities (see Table 5.2).

Nevertheless, even in the New Economy a stock market decline is not a sufficient indicator that the boom is about to

Table 5.2   The Tech Cycle and the Stock Market

On the Upside	*On the Downside*
Rapid innovation boosts earnings and stimulates the formation of new companies	Slower innovation reduces earnings growth
Increasing-returns-to-scale firms show rising productivity as their markets and the economy grow	Increasing-returns-to-scale firms have falling profit margins as the economy weakens
Less fear of market setbacks and recessions lowers the required risk premium	Investors get more worried as the economy and market fall, and demand higher risk premiums
Low inflation boosts stock prices	Rising inflation erodes equity prices

come to an end. Stock prices bounce around far too much, for too many reasons, to ever be reliable signals by themselves, even in the New Economy.

It's also essential to focus directly on spending on technology. Business spending on information technology has a momentum separate from the stock market. Companies set their information technology budgets based on a combination of falling prices, perception of value, and the fear that someone else is going to win if they don't keep investing in technology. They are constantly weighing the value of a dollar spent on technology against the value of the same dollar spent on something else. So if spending on technology starts to slow or even drop over a period of some months, that's another sign that the pace of innovation that has sustained the New Economy is starting to flag as well.

Thus, a clear signal that the New Economy boom is about to come undone would be a substantial and extended fall in the Nasdaq combined with a significant slowdown in tech spending. Together these would indicate that the leading sector of the economy is losing strength.

Pragmatically, what does this mean? What should you look

for? A reasonable measure of the stock market's health would be the three-month moving average of the Nasdaq composite stock index. As we saw in Chapter 4, the movements of the Nasdaq are reasonably well correlated with venture capital funding, one of the key motive forces for the New Economy. Moreover, the Nasdaq index reflects how investors assess the future of the tech sector.

For technology spending, a decent leading indicator is the three-month moving average of orders for information technology equipment, published monthly by the Census Bureau. There are other tech indicators, of course. The Semiconductor Industry Association publishes a monthly survey of semiconductor sales globally, and research companies such as International Data Corporation collect information on sales of personal computers. Nevertheless, the Census data, because they track orders, have the most value as a leading indicator.

A red flag would be a sustained and simultaneous decline in both orders and stock prices. Between 1995 and the middle of 2000, there have been times when the moving average of tech orders have fallen for two months in a row. There have also been times when the moving average of the Nasdaq index has fallen as many as three months in a row. But so far they have never coincided.

As of mid-summer, 2000, the Nasdaq is about 25% below its high, reached earlier this year. If and when tech orders fall as well, that will be a clear indication that the boom is weakening, and that the slide may be about to begin.

TECHNOLOGY PRICES AND INNOVATION

Stocks and tech spending are not the only signs of an impeding tech slowdown—prices are an important indicator as well. But the key measure is not the overall inflation rate, but the rate at which the prices of information technology equipment and software are falling.

The price of information processing has consistently declined since the invention of the microprocessor. Whether defined by their speed or by the number of transistors on a chip, the power of microprocessors has grown steadily over the past twenty years or so, and that has been reflected in falling prices.

Nevertheless, a hallmark of the New Economy boom has been an amazing acceleration of the rate of price decreases. Between 1995 and 1999, the price of computer equipment bought by businesses declined at a rate of roughly 24% per year. That's almost twice as fast as the 13% annual rate of decline between 1980 and 1995.[1] Prices for the broader category of information technology goods—including computers, communications equipment, and software—show much the same pattern, with a much faster decline in the second half of the 1990s compared to the earlier period.

It's a mistake to view the faster declines of recent years as a purely technological phenomenon. The New Economy boom provided financial incentives to get new technology to market faster, which helped push down prices for existing products. The unceasing flow of venture capital spawned small, innovative startups, while companies such as Microsoft, Intel, and Cisco accelerated their development of new versions of software and hardware in response.

Any sustained moderation in the rate of price declines for information technology goods—or even the beginning of price increases—would be a sign that an essential element of the New Economy boom was disappearing. In the first half of 2000 the price of information technology goods bought by businesses actually rose, the first time that has happened since the beginning of 1991. If this trend continues, it may indicate that the tech decline is about to start.

THE ROLE OF NONTECH INDUSTRIES

Why such a big emphasis on the behavior of the technology sector? After all, despite the attention devoted to the information revolution, the technology industries are a relatively small share of the economy. In the first quarter of 2000, the information technology components of GDP accounted for only $600 billion (at an annual rate), or about 6% of output.[2] By comparison, more than $1 trillion was spent on medical care alone.

But, in fact, the information technology sector has an influence far out of proportion to its size. The increase in IT spending is so rapid that it accounts for an extremely high share of growth of GDP, industrial production, the market value of the stock market, and wages. In other words, the tech boom is supporting a large proportion of economic activity through a variety of diverse channels—and when the tech cycle turns down, a lot of apparently unrelated consumer and business spending will melt away as well.

Look first at the direct impact of the IT sector on GDP and industrial production. Since 1995 the IT sector has accounted for roughly 25% of GDP growth (Figure 5.1). Its share of the growth in manufacturing is even larger. From June 1999 to June 2000, computers, semiconductors, and communications equipment accounted for roughly three-quarters of the growth in manufacturing production.

And these numbers, although large, actually understate the impact of the technology sector on the economy. Tech companies have been generating enormous amounts of cash, in the form of wages, profits, stock options, capital gains, and the like. All of that money wends its way through the economy in the form of spending on autos, homes, vacations, and all the luxury items on which people spend money when times are good.

Consider the famed "wealth effect," for example. Federal Reserve Chairman Alan Greenspan has attributed much of the

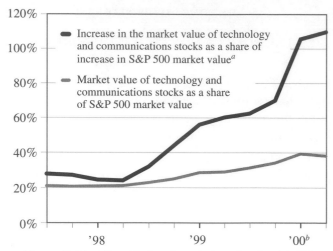

Figure 5.1A   How Technology Drives the Wealth Effect.
Sources: Standard & Poor's; author calculations.
[a]Compared to a year earlier.
[b]First and second quarters only.

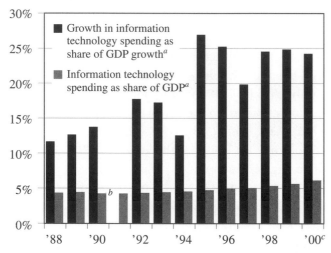

Figure 5.1B   How Technology Drives Economic Growth.
Sources: Bureau of Economic Analysis; author calculations.
[a]Business spending on information technology equipment
and software, consumer spending on computers and telecom services,
and government spending on computers, adjusted for foreign trade.
[b]The whole economy shrunk in 1991.
[c]Based on change in the first quarter of 2000 compared to a year earlier.

exceptional growth in consumer spending in recent years to the impact of rising stock prices. As the market value of assets goes up, Greenspan warned in February 2000, that creates "additional purchasing power for which no additional goods or services have yet been produced."[3] The more Wall Street goes up, the more Americans are willing to spend.

But, in fact, most of the wealth effect—and the shopping spree that comes with it—is due primarily to the soaring price of technology stocks. From the second quarter of 1999 to the second quarter of 2000, the tech sector, including the telephone companies, was responsible for *all* of the increase in market value of the S&P 500 (Figure 5.1). That's despite the fall of the Internet stocks in early 2000.

Looking back a bit farther, between the middle of 1995 and the middle of 2000, about 45% of the rise in the market value of the S&P 500 came from the tech sector. Just four companies— Intel, Microsoft, Cisco, and America Online—were responsible for more than a $1 trillion increase in market value over that five-year period.

But that's only part of it. The tech companies have been the source of a surprisingly large portion of the wage gains in the economy as well. Payrolls have exploded for tech companies. Meanwhile, wages for tech-related jobs has been soaring for everyone—from managers and programmers to the management consultants who put in new information systems to the receptionists greeting visitors at software companies. On the other hand, the real wage gains in many nontech industries have been comparatively meager. For example, real hourly wages for nonsupervisory workers in the grocery store industry peaked in 1998, and have actually been falling since then.[4] Similarly, pay increases have been weak in much of manufacturing, construction, and the service sector, outside of tech-related jobs.

As a result, when the tech boom ends, there will not be much to support consumer spending. Tech stocks will fall and tech pay will stop rising—and there is no evidence that the rest of the economy will be able to pick up the slack.

THE AUTOMOBILE CRASH

The closest historical precedent is the behavior of auto sales and stocks in the months before the crash of 1929. In terms of its importance to the economy and the market, the automotive industry in the 1920s was the equivalent of today's high-tech sector. The tripling of auto production was the single biggest force for growth in the 1920s, and it helped drive a similar expansion in related industries such as steel, rubber, and highway construction. The Standard & Poor's index for automobile stocks more than tripled between the beginning of 1926 and the spring of 1929, far outpacing the doubling of the market as a whole.[5]

In retrospect, the first precursor of the coming storm was a simultaneous slowdown in auto production in the spring of 1929 and a fall in the auto stocks. After peaking in April 1929, factory production of passenger cars slid by 41% over the next six months. Few economists or corporate executives were concerned, because they had seen similar slides in the auto market before. Production had fallen by 40% or more in the second halves of both 1927 and 1928, only to bounce back even bigger than before.

But never had a slide in auto production been accompanied by a similar downtrend in the price of auto stocks, which peaked in March 1929 and then fell 15% by September 1929. That was not normal behavior. Auto stocks had risen at an average of almost 50% per year for the previous three years, with only the briefest of pauses.

Investors reacted to the drop in auto stocks by shifting into other stocks. At the time this "market rotation" was applauded as a sign of strength in the economy. "At a moment when many

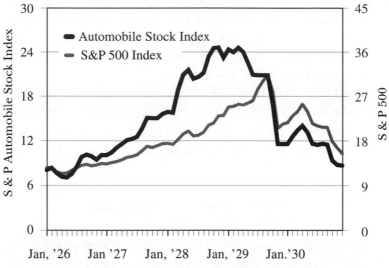

Figure 5.2A   The Run-Up to the Crash, 1926–1930.

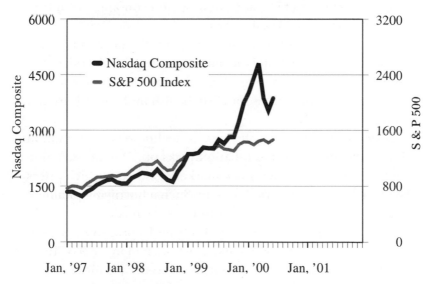

Figure 5.2B   The Run-Up to the Crash, 1997–?
Sources: Standard & Poor's, DRI/McGraw-Hill.

of the high-flyers of earlier months were losing ground, the really sensational advances were being made by shares of such solid and conservatively managed companies as United States Steel, General Electric, and American Telephone," wrote Frederick Lewis Allen in *Only Yesterday*.[6]

What investors did not realize, however, was that the falloff in auto sales and auto stocks was a sign that the leading sector of the economy, the one that had driven growth, was faltering. And that, in turn, was a sign that the boom was near its end.

THE CALM BEFORE THE STORM

Historically, there is an interval "between the end of euphoria and the onset of what classic writers called revulsion and discredit,"[7] in the words of Charles Kindleberger. This is the calm before the storm—a period of general uneasiness, followed first by a stock market crash, and then by an economic downturn. The whole process takes time to unfold.

There was a gap of six months between the peak of automobile sales in April 1929 and the market crash of Black Friday. The same thing could happen again, as investors slowly come to realize that their expectations for high growth and low risk are not going to be fulfilled.

Imagine the scenario: the rate of technological innovation slows, demand slows, and inflation picks up. One possible outcome would be a sudden stock market decline, in which prices fall over a very short period of time. Such a horrifying plummet is the stuff of which investor nightmares are made.

But the long, slow slide to the Internet Depression need not be marked by the sort of one-day crash we had in 1929 or 1987. Instead, the experience could be closer to the Japanese case of 1990, when the Nikkei fell by nearly 50% from its high at the beginning of the year to its low without dropping more than 7% in any particular day.

Even after the market starts its descent—whether it be rapid or drawn-out—there will be a substantial lag before it hits the economy. While a plunging market may have an immediate negative effect on the ability of young firms to float stock offerings, history suggests that it takes at least a year for the stock market to affect venture capital flows.

The loss of stock market wealth may also take quite a while to pull down consumer spending. In the long run, economists generally believe that reducing household wealth by a dollar would cut spending by 3 cents to 5 cents. That means a fall in the Dow from 11,000 to 8500, say, would cut household wealth by at least $4 trillion, eventually reducing consumption by between $120 billion and $200 billion.[8] But in the short run, according to a 1999 study by two economists from the Federal Reserve Bank of New York, it is hard to use the wealth effect to predict changes in spending patterns. As the Fed economists wrote: "Forecasts of future consumption growth are not typically improved by taking changes in existing wealth into account."[9]

Finally, long booms create a psychological momentum that is tough to break, even after a crash. When investors have experienced a long boom punctuated by short declines that are quickly reversed, they are conditioned to associate negative events with future gains—they buy on the dips. It takes a long time to extinguish this conditioning. History suggests that it takes a year or more of steady declines for investors to realize that the market is not coming back again.

This was the experience after the crash of 1929. Investors had seen the market plunge several times in the previous decade, including a 30% drop in 1921 and a 19% decline in 1924. In late 1929, there was the feeling that once again the market and the economy were going to bounce right back. The market crash was even thought to have some beneficial side-effects, as *Business Week* noted in its December 25, 1929 issue:

> Another important result of the Wall Street upheaval is the release of highly-paid executives from close contact with stock brokers. Time spent in telephoning orders and discussing futures, and in worrying about the antics of stocks, can now be devoted to running a plant, which is really a full-time job.[10]

The optimistic tone lasted well into 1930. In the spring of that year, there were clear signs that things were improving. In early April, the S&P index was actually up by as much as 5% over a year earlier. (The Dow Jones Industrial Index had a strong rebound also, but never actually got above its level a year earlier.) "On May 1, President Hoover stated that the United States was not through its difficulties but that he was convinced that the country had passed the worst," wrote Kindleberger.[11] Noted economic historian Peter Temin, "People responded to the fall of business activity and prices in 1930 in roughly the same way they reacted to the roughly similar fall in 1921. They knew business was bad, but they expected it to recover soon."[12]

In fact, the manufacturing sector did start to come back. In April 1930, the production of consumer goods, except autos, was only slightly below where it had been a year earlier. Production of electric power and chemicals was up compared to the previous year, and freight car shipments were up 71%. The only signs of real weakness were in auto production and related industries such as steel.

Many people interpreted the period as a needed break from the speculative excesses. By summer, there was a feeling that things were turning up. In early July 1930, *Business Week* reported that "the underlying forces are beginning to turn in the direction of recovery."[13] And on the cover of its August 20, 1930 issue, the magazine said: "There is reason to believe the worst is over—that recovery has begun; that it will be rapid as compared with recovery in 1921."[14]

THE POLICY DESERT

The aftermath of a stock market crash is the period when major policy and investment mistakes are made. The market has collapsed but the economy still looks strong, deterring the central bank from pumping more money into the system. Indeed, this is when the inflation hawks call for raising rates.

These sorts of misjudgments are not a relic of the 1930s. Just look at what happened in Japan in the early 1990s. In 1990, the Nikkei stock index fell by almost half, but business investment continued to rise at double-digit rates. Corporate capital spending didn't peak until early 1991, and actually stayed at high levels until early 1992.

At the time, the conventional wisdom was that the worst problem facing Japan was high inflation and high housing prices. "It is time for the Bank of Japan to raise interest rates again," opined *The Economist* in May 1990. "There is little chance that Japan's financial traumas will seriously hamper the Japanese economy or Japanese industry."[15] In November 1990, Motohiko Sasaki, chief economist at Sumitomo Trust & Banking Co., said, "Japan's economy is still booming."[16] As late as December 1990, the governor of the Bank of Japan was saying that business conditions remained strong—a misjudgment that helped lead to excessively tight monetary policy and the ten-year stagnation of the Japanese economy.[17]

Of course, the U.S. has a very different economy from Japan's. But during the transition between the boom and the bust, it's easy for policymakers and investors to make mistakes that have grave consequences—especially in times when their long-standing assumptions about the economy no longer accord so well with reality.

CHAPTER SIX

The Next Depression

So far I have laid out the early stages of the tech cycle down-turn. What's been left open, though, is the critical question for workers, for investors, and for managers: How bad will the down-turn be?

After nearly a decade of prosperity, most households and busi-nesses have built up enough of a cushion to ride out a short downturn. But if the downturn stretches out and gets longer and deeper, the appropriate strategy changes. Smart investors shift from equities to less risky investments, households pull back on spending, businesses cut capital investment and hiring, and everybody hunkers down for the long haul.

If the U.S. economy was still primarily based on manufactur-ing, we could be confident that any downturn would be relatively short and controlled. Economists have spent the past seventy years learning how to control the booms and busts of industrial economies, and are justifiably proud of this achievement.

But the world doesn't stand still. The U.S. has a New Economy in which the business cycle has been replaced by the tech cycle, fueled by risk capital and an intense devotion to innovation. In principle, there's no reason why economic policymakers cannot learn to manage the tech cycle as well as they did the business

cycle. But the problem is deeper than simply a lack of knowledge. On an intellectual level, economists—in Washington, on
Wall Street, in academics—are willing to talk about the importance of computers and the Internet. But in their hearts many
do not accept that anything really significant has changed. As a
result, policymakers will continue to treat technological change
as if it were separate from the rest of the economy.

What's worse, a fair number of influential policymakers and
economists still believe the New Economy is a mirage and that
the 1990s were not a decade of prosperity but a speculative bubble. They will welcome a downturn—even a steep one—as the
natural and necessary response to the excesses of the 1990s.

All things considered, there is a good chance that the U.S. is
on the road to a severe recession or even depression. As happened in the 1930s in the U.S. and the 1990s in Japan, policymakers, doing what they think is right, are on the brink of making a fundamental mistake: the decision to manage the economy
as if technology did not matter.

A DIFFERENT KIND OF DEPRESSION

The term "depression" has a vaguely musty air to it, like something left over from a different era. For the most part, economics textbooks generally treat the topic of depression as if it were
solely a matter for historians, never to happen again. Indeed, it
is unlikely that the desperation of the 1930s, with a 25% unemployment rate, falling prices, and shuttered banks, will ever be
repeated.

But the unlikelihood of a 1930s-style catastrophe does not
rule out a different kind of paralyzing and long-lasting downturn—one that would also merit being called a depression. An
Internet Depression, if and when it comes, will not be centered
in the automobile and steel factories that led the economy into

the Great Depression. Rather, the Internet Depression will hit hardest at the new information technology and communications industries that drove growth in the 1990s. And just as the hallmark of the New Economy has been an accelerated rate of technological innovation, so the pain of the Internet Depression will be felt as a dramatic and pervasive lowering of our expectations for future growth.

In effect, a depression is a recession that is not followed by a quick, genuine recovery. Much like a depressed person, the economy does not easily regain its former buoyancy and vigor.[1] People adjust to the depressed economy, and pessimism about the future begins to seem normal, leading to less investment, less risk-taking, and even more depressed growth in the future. If policymakers let the depression go on too long, the economy gets stuck on a slow growth path that is difficult to escape. At that point, depression becomes the norm—and that would be the biggest disaster of all.

Harry Truman said, "Recession is when your neighbor loses his job; depression is when you lose yours" (a line later borrowed by Ronald Reagan). But that's not quite right. In the New Economy, it's better to say "A recession is when your neighbor loses his job; a depression is when it takes him a long time to get another one." The economy falls substantially below its potential and stays there.

It is possible to have a growth depression, when the economy creeps along, but falls further and further below its potential output. The clearest example of a growth depression is Japan in the 1990s. The Japanese economy grew at a 1.3% average rate during the decade, but only because the government poured enormous amounts of money into propping it up. Even with that, industrial production, corporate profits, and business investment were all lower in 1999 than they had been in 1990. By the end of the decade, Japan's economy was roughly 20% smaller than it would have been if productivity had grown at the rate of the 1970s and 1980s.

To put it a different way, a recession is like a motor running out of fuel, while a depression is like a badly damaged car that needs to be repaired before it can run again. Once an economy has sunk into a depression, it is difficult to restart it without making structural and institutional changes.

THE THEORY OF THE SECOND MISTAKE

Recessions are inevitable in any economy, New, Old, or indifferent. Investment booms can be followed by busts. Policymakers can make mistakes—for instance, by raising interest rates too much or too little.

But that's not what causes depressions. Depressions happen when policymakers—for reasons that seem perfectly good at the time—continue to pursue deflationary policies even after the economy has gone into recession. In other words, it's the *second* mistake that kills the economy.

Depressions are much more likely when an economy is in transition—when the old institutions and rules don't fit anymore. That's when policymakers are most likely to draw the wrong conclusions about what policy to follow.

The Great Depression, according to the economic historian Peter Temin, can be thought of as "two (or more) recessions coming on top of one another."[2] The first recession, precipitated by the stock market crash of 1929, was the natural follow-on to the boom of the 1920s. After a decade of soaring stock prices, auto purchases, and home building, some sort of a slump is almost inevitable.

But the second recession, which started in 1931, was iatrogenic—a "doctor-induced illness." The Federal Reserve, following the policies it thought was right at the time, raised rates sharply in October 1931, stomping an already weak domestic and global economy into the ground. By Temin's estimates, the second recession accounted for fully two-thirds of the output lost from the Depression.[3]

Why would the Fed raise rates? It thought it was doing the right thing. The point of higher interest rates was to defend the gold standard—that is, to slow the rush of gold leaving the country. The Fed worried that *not* raising rates would have all sorts of negative consequences, from runaway inflation to a collapse of the world financial system. As Eichengreen and Temin note, "maintenance of the gold standard would in time restore employment, central bankers thought, while attempts to increase employment directly would fail."[4]

The Federal Reserve strategy was supported by many of the prominent economists of the time, who believed that the right approach to the slump was to cut wages, jobs, and prices until the economy returned to a more sustainable level. There was an almost moralistic sense among many economists and policy-makers that a deep recession was a healthy and necessary antidote to the speculative excesses of the 1920s. In the aftermath of the stock market crash of 1929, Andrew Mellon, Treasury Secretary under Hoover, made the well-known statement:

> Liquidate labor, liquidate stocks, liquidate the farmers, liquidate real estate . . . it will purge the rottenness out of the system. High costs of living and high living will come down. People will work harder, live a more moral life. Values will be adjusted, and enterprising people will pick up the wrecks from less competent people.[5]

A July 1930 editorial in *Business Week* inveighed against what it called the "castor-oil school of economics":

> One of the most depressing things about this business depression . . . is the way the fatalists and bitter-enders have returned to power and influence over business thinking. . . .
>
> [there is] a savage insistence upon the inexorable necessity that an errant and self-indulgent business community shall take its medicine, and plenty of it; that it shall suffer, by Jupiter, without relief or palliative till it has learned its lesson,

whatever that is; that, having danced on Sunday in violation
of the blue-laws of the economics of original sin, it shall pay
the piper.

The only way business can recover . . . [they say] . . . is by a
prolonged and painful purging process. . . . No matter how
long it takes or how much the patient suffers, nature must be
allowed to take her course.[6]

Three months later, the editors of *Business Week* conceded
defeat:

The deflationists are in the saddle. The events of the past
month have driven home the fact that they have now completely unhorsed not only the New Era enthusiasts of yester-
year, but the majority of the level-headed intelligent business
minds of the country. . . . For some reason, to this type of mind,
inflation enjoys a monopoly of evil and sums up all the economic sins.[7]

The Fed pursued tight money policies until well into 1933, as
did most central banks in Europe. The global economy did not
start to recover until central bankers gave up defending the gold
standard and started pursuing policies designed to pump up
economies rather than deflate them.

STEERING THE OLD ECONOMY

The Federal Reserve would not make the same second mistake
today. The Keynesian lesson, as applied to an industrial economy, is clear. Faced with clear signs of deflation and contracting
demand, the duty of the central bank is to pump liquidity into
the economy until it revives.

In fact, economists over the past seventy years have evolved a
fairly simple set of rules for monetary policy: keep the level of
utilization of labor and capital high enough that the economy

feels prosperous, but low enough that inflation does not start accelerating. If inflation starts accelerating, then the Fed raises interest rates and slows the economy until unemployment rises and capacity utilization of factories falls. Conversely, if unemployment is too high, the Fed cuts rates until the economy accelerates again.

This vision of policy is often translated into the notion that the economy has a speed limit. The image is one of the economy as a car, where the driver alternately taps the brake and the gas pedal to keep the car moving at a reasonable speed. The goal is to maintain a happy medium—not so fast that the car overheats and starts to rattle, and not so slow that the passengers start to complain.

These rules don't stop the Fed from making honest mistakes as driving conditions change. The exact speed at which the economy can grow and the precise level of unemployment that will trigger inflation have changed repeatedly. Moreover, the economy is often buffeted by unexpected events, like the oil price increases of the 1970s, the stock market crash of 1987, the Gulf War in 1990, and the East Asian collapse of 1997. New technologies arise, existing ones falter. These bumps and curves in the road, coming without warning, make it much harder to judge what the right policy should be.

Nevertheless, most macroeconomists now agree on the basic principles of monetary policy. Even the unexpected New Economy boom of the 1990s did not shake the consensus. More than four years of rapid growth without inflation were interpreted as a shift to a higher speed limit, not a change in the basic rules for driving the economy. Indeed, the conventional wisdom among many policymakers and economists in the late 1990s and into 2000 was that the U.S. did not have a New Economy, but the same economy growing at a faster sustainable rate—a kind of "Old Economy Plus." As Federal Reserve Board Governor Larry Meyer said in a November 1999 speech, "The key message is that old rules still apply to the new limits."[8] Or as two University of

California economists put it in their best-selling 1999 book, *Information Rules,* "Technology changes. Economic laws do not."[9]

But as institutions change, so do the appropriate rules for running them. If central bankers and economists continue to insist that the New Economy is governed by the old institutions and the old rules, then the odds that a recession will turn into an Internet Depression go up.

FLYING THE NEW ECONOMY

In the Old Economy there is little connection between the underlying rate of technological change and the rest of the economy. So the Federal Reserve can raise interest rates without worrying that putting on the brakes will undermine the forces of technological progress.

But in the New Economy, that's not true anymore. The incentives for innovation are closely tied to the stock market and economic growth. Without a strong equity market, the flow of venture capital and IPO funds drics up. As the economy slows and the market dips, there is less pressure for the creation and adoption of new ideas. Productivity growth slows, and inflation rises.

Unless they realize this, the Federal Reserve might make several serious policy mistakes. First, a monetary policy aimed at holding down the stock market—as the Fed seemed to be following in 2000—runs the risk of cutting off one of the major sources of technology growth. Federal Reserve Chairman Alan Greenspan argued repeatedly in 1999 and 2000 that a high stock market was fueling excess consumer demand. He seemed to give far less weight, however, to the stock market's effects on innovation.

Second, raising rates in response to higher inflation may be exactly the wrong thing to do. True, the laws of supply and demand have not been repealed. Rising prices and wages can be a sign of an overheated economy, just as they were in the past.

But there's an important factor operating in the New Economy that was not present in the Old Economy. As the tech cycle turns down, the availability of startup capital for new businesses shrinks and the rate of technological and business innovation slows. Thus, existing companies face less competition from new firms just as the flow of productivity-enhancing innovation falls off. The combination makes it both easier and more essential for companies to raise prices.

Thus, in its initial stages the tech downturn could very well be accompanied by a surge of "suppressed" inflation. Companies that have been trying to raise prices for years will finally be able to do so, especially if they want to maintain profits. As a result, a monetary policy aimed only at suppressing inflation runs the risk of raising rates at a time when the IPO and venture capital markets are already staggering.

Third, the old rules underestimate just how far and how fast the economy can drop. In the Old Economy, a steady rate of technological innovation provided a floor underneath growth. If technological change boosts productivity by 2% each year, say, then the economy will tend to grow by that amount even if employment is not increasing. In the New Economy, that floor isn't there anymore. The rate of technological change goes down as the economy slows.

The bottom line is that the Fed has to be as concerned with innovation as it is with demand. To put it a different way, if the Old Economy is a car, the New Economy is more like an airplane. Planes travel faster and farther than cars do, with more powerful engines. But more important, pilots have to be aware that airplanes operate in a third dimension.

For the New Economy, that third dimension is the rate of technological and business innovation. Just as decisions made by the pilot of a plane affect its altitude as well as its speed, the actions of the central bank affect the pace of innovation, through the financial markets and, more particularly, the incentives for the formation of innovative new businesses.

On the one hand, the New Economy can grow rapidly without inflation, soaring faster and higher than the Old Economy, because growth and strong stock markets stimulate innovation. For the passengers, the ride is exhilarating. They are going faster and farther than they ever have before—4% to 5% growth annually, 20% increases in the stock market. There are bumps—big ones, sometimes—but the plane keeps flying. And as the passengers look out the window, they see the cars crawling slowly below.

But the flip side is that the New Economy can fall farther and harder than the Old Economy. Technological and business innovation is a high-risk, high-return process that operates best when the economy runs hotter. Venture capital, the formation of innovative new businesses, the mobile labor force—all require a certain minimum rate of economic growth to function correctly. It's far easier to start an Amazon.com or an eBay in an economy that is growing, and where the stock market is strong.

Unlike the Old Economy, the New Economy has a stall speed. Any airplane, whether a Boeing 747 or a small Cessna, needs to maintain enough speed to stay in the air. Slowing a plane below the stall speed, while attempting to maintain level flight, can have serious consequences. Federal Aviation Administration guidelines for pilot training state: "If an airplane's speed is too slow . . . the result is a separation of airflow from the wing, loss of lift, a large increase in drag, and eventually a stall."[10] If the plane is too low when the stall occurs, the outcome can be a bad crash.

But when the plane stalls and starts to plummet, only a trained pilot will know that the right response may well be to push down the nose and add more power. By contrast, someone who has only driven a car will react to a stall by trying to pull the nose of the plane up, which only slows the plane further and makes a crash more likely.

Similarly, policymakers have to be aware that it is possible that slowing productivity and rising inflation may reflect a squeeze in the risk capital markets, not an excess of demand over supply. Raising interest rates, like raising the nose of a stalled plane, will have the effect of further cutting off the flow of funds to innovative new businesses, making a bad situation much worse. The set of reflexes needed to fly the New Economy may be very different from the ones required to drive the Old Economy.

THE GREENSPAN EFFECT

At this point it is appropriate to pause and offer words of praise for Alan Greenspan. Despite having spent his entire adult life studying the ins and outs of the Old Economy, despite opposition from within the Fed, and despite his worries about the stock market, Greenspan was able to embrace the idea that the U.S. was undergoing an information revolution, and that the economy could grow faster, more safely, than it had in the past. In a July 2000 speech entitled "Structural Change in the New Economy," Greenspan observed that

> information technologies have begun to alter significantly how we do business and create economic value, often in ways that were not foreseeable even a decade ago. . . . One result of the more-rapid pace of IT innovation has been a visible acceleration of the process that noted economist Joseph Schumpeter many years ago termed "creative destruction"— the continuous shift in which emerging technologies push out the old.[11]

Because of his understanding that the economy has changed, Greenspan has been able, in effect, to get the New Economy plane off the ground and into level flight—without the equivalent of pilot training. This achievement should not be minimized. Few if any other economists would have felt confident enough to allow the economy to roll even as unemployment dropped to 4%, far below the level which was thought to trigger inflation.

Because of his track record, it is possible that Greenspan will be able to slow the New Economy to a manageable speed without stalling it out or allowing it to spin into depression. That would involve slight increases in interest rates, but not enough to ruin the IPO market and the flow of new companies.

But keeping the New Economy flying—especially if it runs into economic turbulence—may be tougher than getting it into the air. Not even Greenspan has experienced a New Economy bust, making it difficult for him to act quickly and correctly should things go bad. Moreover, there is still no consensus among policymakers about the nature of the boom—and these disagreements, too, will slow any reactions in a crisis.

THE TECHNO-PESSIMISTS

The problem is not simply that the Fed may make an honest mistake in assessing policy. What's more worrisome are the people who, if the New Economy plane starts to fall, will say it should never have been up in the sky at all. That group includes the bears who believed the stock market boom of the 1990s to be a bubble, and the die-hard "techno-pessimists" who considered the New Economy nothing but illusion fueled by speculation and a few special factors.

At base, these skeptics believed, whether they said so explicitly or not, that the Internet and computers were minor-league technologies that did not measure up to such past breakthroughs such as electricity, the internal combustion engine, and the railroad. At various times the Internet revolution was belittled by economists, who called it no more important than air conditioning (which made it far easier to move jobs to hot climates), direct-dial long-distance calling, and freight containerization (which made freight transportation more efficient by reducing the number of times that goods needed to be handled). Paul Krugman, one of the most persistent critics of the New Economy, wrote in June 1998: "The truth is that we live in an age not of extraordinary progress but of technological disappointment."[12]

Even as late as 1999, after the U.S. had racked up several years of strong productivity gains, the New Economy skeptics still refused to admit that anything fundamental had changed. The U.S. was maybe growing a bit faster, with a bit more technology, but it was still the same economy, following the same rules.

For example, in May 2000, Robert J. Gordon of Northwestern University, a leading macroeconomist and one of the most articulate critics of the New Economy, wrote:

> computers and the internet do not measure up to the Great Inventions of the late nineteenth and early twentieth century. . . . Even derivatives of electricity like the air conditioner are probably more valued by the consumer, at least in the southern half of the United States, than the invention of the Internet.[13]

And in an April 2000 column, Robert Samuelson, the well-known economics columnist for the *Washington Post,* wrote: "Almost everything that's supposed to be 'new' about the New Economy has happened before."[14]

The downside of the tech cycle will give these pessimists a chance to say, "I told you so." More important, their preferred policy response to a recession will be to let the economy fall back to what they consider a "sustainable" level of output. Like the deflationists of the Great Depression, the pessimists will favor letting the economy and the market plunge in order to wring out the speculative excesses.

FISCAL MISSTEPS

So far we have mostly focused on the monetary policy mistakes that could lead to the Internet Depression. That's because most economists agree that when it comes to preventing (or causing) depression, monetary policy is a far more important tool than fiscal policy. Nevertheless, running an expansive fiscal policy— opening up the spending spigots and cutting taxes—is essential for fighting a deep recession.

Unfortunately, maintaining a balanced budget has become a central tenet of both political parties, which they will fight to maintain even as the economy slides and revenues fall. Indeed, the Democratic candidate for president, Al Gore, told the *Wall Street Journal* in January 2000 that he would cut spending if the economy slows, "just as a corporation has to cut expenses if revenues fall off."[15]

But such policies take us down the rocky path followed by Herbert Hoover, who aggressively pursued a balanced budget until he was voted out of office in 1932. Hoover was not stupid— he thought he was doing the right thing, and he was supported by well-known economists and by Congress. Wrote one historian:

> The general opinion was that cutbacks in government spending were necessary to break out of the slump and get the business cycle moving again.[16]

> When shrinking federal revenues resulting from the depression caused the government to run at a deficit, Hoover forgot about trying to stimulate consumer spending. He called for tax increases and reduced government outlays in order to balance the budget. In 1932, as the depression sounded the depths, Congress *raised* taxes by a larger percentage than ever before in American history.[17]

It wasn't just the U.S. that went down the wrong road. Germany, France, and Britain all tried to balance their budgets in the face of the depression. In Britain, a committee headed by the insurance executive Sir George May recommended in August 1931 reduced spending for social services, steep pay cuts for teachers, soldiers, and policemen, and the postponement of some public works projects.[18]

Of course, we couldn't be this stupid again, could we? Nobody would have predicted that the Japanese government would increase taxes in 1997, when their economy was still struggling. But they did, with the best of intentions—and with the result of pushing Japan back into recession again.

THE COMING FORECASTING FIASCO

At this point skeptical economists will vehemently disagree. Sure, they will say, innovative small firms are important. But in a $9 trillion economy, $100 billion in venture capital is relatively insignificant, no matter how much innovation comes out of it. Even if venture capital and the whole tech sector falls, that's not enough to send the economy into depression. Moreover, if the economy does start to slip into a deep recession or depression, the Federal Reserve will see it coming in time to lower rates.

These counterarguments really boil down to two assertions. First, economists understand recessions well enough to judge which shocks will cause downturns and which ones won't. Second, the signs of an impending deep recession are clear enough that the Federal Reserve and Congress can make the appropriate policy responses.

This confidence is completely unwarranted, since historical evidence does not support either assertion. Even before the New Economy, economic forecasters consistently missed the beginnings of most recessions and badly underestimated the length and depth of recessions once they started.

Moreover, there are several reasons to believe that this long-time tendency to underestimate the chances for steep declines will become even more prevalent in the New Economy. First, the official data are missing more and more of the real activity in the economy, making it hard to tell what is happening, even as it takes place. Second, the shift to an increasing-returns-to-scale economy will make the swings in growth both bigger and less predictable by conventional macroeconomic models. Just as economists consistently underestimated the positive impact of risk capital and innovation during the boom of the 1990s, they will underestimate the negative effects on the downside of the tech cycle as well.

Let's start with the track record of forecasters, which is nothing to boast about. Even after a downturn has started, forecasters consistently underestimate how bad it will get and how long it will last. In most recessions, they can't even get the direction of the economy right. For example, the oil price shock of October 1973 helped set off a deep recession starting in December 1973, the steepest downturn since the Great Depression. When they were asked in December 1973 how they expected the economy to do in the next year, the consensus forecast was for output to rise by 1.4% in 1974. In fact, it fell, by 2.1%.[19] As *Business Week* reported in December 1974, the forecasts were so embarrassing that the chief economist for Morgan Guaranty Trust said that

> we've decided that economic forecasting is so deficient that we're not going to perpetuate any more confusion. There is something misleading about giving people what purport to be accurate numbers when they are really no such thing.[20]

The forecasts for the duration and depth of the recession that started in July 1981 were if anything even farther off the mark. In October 1981, most economists were anticipating a "relatively mild recession." In December, with the recession five months old, the consensus forecast for 1982 was for a 2.9% gain in output.[21] Instead, the economy crashed in the second half of 1982, falling by 1.7% for the year. Once again, the forecasters got the direction wrong and missed a very deep recession.

Twenty years of economic research since then have not improved the accuracy of forecasts. In the late 1980s, two leading econometricians, James Stock and Mark Watson, used the most advanced statistical techniques available to construct a new way of predicting recessions. Unfortunately, their new 'experimental recession index' failed to forecast the 1990–91 downturn.

The Asian crisis of 1997 gave economists another chance to show the limitations of their models. Not only was the crisis itself not forecasted, but even after it started forecasters completely missed the depth of the damage to the Asian economies. For example, the forecasts done in January 1998 badly underestimated the massive drop in investment and exports resulting from the crisis.

This inability to predict economic disasters is built into the structure of all major forecasting models. As I mentioned in the previous chapter, they all assume a steady flow of technological change, which puts a floor under growth. Moreover, the models are intentionally designed so that a small change in any economic variable can have only a small impact on the rest of the economy. As a result, unless you plug in a large increase in interest rates or a major economic catastrophe—oil prices rising to $60 a barrel for a year, say, or the stock market dropping by 40%—the models will almost never predict a recession.

A STABLE ECONOMY?

Is there any reason to think economists will do any better forecasting the next recession? Quite the opposite. One reason is that more and more economic activity is in industries that are poorly measured by the official data. Manufacturing is well covered, but many of the information industries are not. The Federal Reserve, for example, collects information on industrial production and capacity on a monthly basis. But there is simply no comparable timely data for the production and capacity of software or information firms. Yet the level of capacity utilization in software firms is arguably more important to the economy than capacity utilization in manufacturing. If we lack such data, the economy might very well sink into a downturn before any evidence shows up in the official statistics. To put it a different way, we have a speedometer, but no altimeter. We know how fast we are going, but not how high we are.

Moreover, as the economy includes more and more increasing-returns-to-scale industries, it is potentially more sensitive to small shocks. W. Brian Arthur, an economist who was one of the great popularizers of the notion of increasing-returns-to-scale, writes:

> Conventional economic theory is built on the assumption of diminishing returns. Economic actions engender a negative feedback that leads to a predictable equilibrium for prices and market shares. Such feedback tends to stabilize the economy because any major changes will be offset by the very reactions they generate. . . . In many parts of the economy, stabilizing forces appear not to operate. Instead positive feedback magnifies the effects of small economic shifts.[29]

It's important to note that the forecasters and economists who tell us not to worry about a deep recession today are exactly the same people who completely missed predicting the tech-driven boom of the 1990s. On every dimension—jobs, growth,

Table 6.1   Missing the Boom

	Consensus Forecast for GDP Growth (as of December of the prior year)	Reported GDP Growth (as of August of the following year)	Reported GDP Growth (revised, as of August 2000)
1996	1.9	3.3	4.1
1997	2.1	3.8	4.3
1998	2.2	4.3	4.6
1999	1.9	5.0	5.0

Source: Consensus forecast taken from Business Week survey done in December of prior year. GDP growth measured from fourth quarter to fourth quarter.

productivity, investment—they underestimated by far the capabilities of the U.S. economy. For four straight years, from 1996 to 1999, the consensus forecast was within spitting distance of 2%. And every year, growth came in much stronger than expected.

Eventually they learned, at least a little bit: by the end of 1999, most of the forecasters had upped their estimates of growth for 2000 to the 3% to 4% range. But they still kept the same Old Economy models that had produced the bad forecasts in the 1990s.

There's an old saying: fool me once, shame on you—fool me twice, shame on me. The forecasters have already proven that they don't understand the New Economy or the links between the financial markets and innovation. Anyone who puts too much trust in economic forecasts runs the risk of finding out that the forecasts will be as wrong about the magnitude of the downturn as they were about the magnitude of the boom.

CHAPTER SEVEN

Riding Out the Storm

MANY OF THE changes in the economy since the 1930s make the odds of a cataclysmic depression less likely. The government plays a far larger role in the economy than it did in 1929, financial markets are better regulated, and the social safety nets are broader and more pervasive. Perhaps most important, the Federal Reserve has accepted its responsibility as the guarantor of financial stability.

But these stabilizing influences are counteracted by equally potent forces for instability. The financial markets have been pushing out the frontiers of risk, from venture capital to low-equity mortgages. The attachment between workers and companies is becoming increasingly frayed, and pay is becoming more volatile even for full-time employees. Globalization has created the potential for financial crises that are beyond the reach of national regulators.

These opposing forces make forecasting the nature and depth of an Internet Depression exceptionally difficult. Moreover, the course of future major technology breakthroughs is a wild card, unpredictable almost by definition. For example, it's possible that the unraveling of the human genome in early 2000 could be the key to unleashing the full potential of biotechnology. If that happens, it could transform the health care and food industries, and trigger a whole new wave of investment.

For these reasons, the picture of the Internet Depression in this chapter should be regarded as drawn lightly in pencil rather than in permanent ink. Nevertheless, it is possible to discern two basic principles for coping with the tech downturn as it evolves.

First, investors and workers need to realize that the downturn is likely to hit the tech industries first and hardest. Compared to their current rapid growth, the slowdown will feel especially harsh. Nevertheless, the long-term trends that favor information technology industries, investment, and jobs are still in place. Just as the automobile industry was hit hard by the Great Depression but still dominated the postwar economy, so will the high-tech industries face short-term pain and long-term growth.

Second, if the Fed acts quickly enough to staunch the downturn before it gathers speed, then the right thing to do is to make choices assuming that the economy will recover. But if economic policymakers hesitate or pursue the wrong strategy, then it's prudent to plan for the worst. That means pulling back on spending, borrowing, and investing, and taking fewer risks in career choices. Reducing exposure to uncertainty and risk will make it more likely that you will survive the downturn in good shape.

NAVIGATING THE JOB MARKET

As the economy slides into the downside of the tech cycle, how worried should you be about your job? Certainly in the long run the number of information technology–related jobs will continue to climb, just as manufacturing supplanted agriculture in the early part of the 20th century. In general, people who work with computers and the Internet will find jobs more easily than those who do not.

But don't kid yourself: despite the long-term trends, this is going to be a Palm Pilot recession. It will wreak its most devastating damage on the educated, well-paid, computer-literate workers who thought themselves immune from the ups and downs of the economy. Particularly hard hit will be the floating workforce of temporary workers, independent consultants, freelancers, hot programmers, and web designers-for-hire who have thrived in the New Economy boom. These people, who played an essential role during the good times, will find that companies have a lot less need for them when growth, innovation, and risk-taking slow down.

For the past few years, high-tech companies have staffed up under the assumption that the rapid pace of innovation of the late 1990s would continue. But as innovation slows, layoffs will be felt all across the high-tech sector. The first wave was seen already in early 2000, as the dot.coms laid off thousands of workers. But the devastation will stretch from the telecoms to the software makers to the consulting firms.

Why should this be? A technological revolution, such as the one the U.S. is going through now, has two main impacts on hiring. First, by boosting productivity in existing companies, it reduces the number of workers needed in many operations. For example, the advent of voice mail and easy desktop word-processing dramatically reduced the need for secretaries. Between 1995 and 1999, the number of secretaries fell by almost 600,000, or 17%. The number of people processing financial records fell by 74,000. The number of buyers in wholesale and retail trade fell by 16%.

At the same time, the pace of technological change ignited a massive wave of hiring. The ongoing flow of innovation required armies of skilled workers to develop the new generation of products, to staff the new industries, to implement the new technology at existing companies, and to train their workers. That meant companies had to hire programmers able to learn new techniques such as Java and XML quickly, Internet experts who could work with both content and programming tools to build new web sites, and workers who could install and maintain the networks and computer systems that had become so indispensable.

Moreover, the Internet revolution created a tremendous demand for consultants who could help companies assimilate and get the new technology to work properly. Firms such Andersen Consulting, which went from 26,730 employees in 1992 to more than 65,000 in 1999, served as an essential conduit for the technological innovations coming out of the high-tech sector. All told, the number of employees in management consulting firms rose by 40% between 1995 and 1999, making them among the top employers of new college graduates.[1]

During the boom phase of the New Economy, job creation overwhelmed job elimination, as new tech-related jobs came into existence far faster than Old Economy jobs were destroyed. From 1995 to 1999, for example, computer, semiconductor, and communications equipment manufacturers added 75,000 jobs, more than making up for the 57,000 jobs lost in the rest of manufacturing. And the number of employees at software and computer services firms grew by a whopping 700,000 positions.

But a slowing of innovation means a dramatic falloff in the number of people creating new products and companies, which will show up quickly as a cutback in employment at high-tech firms. At the same time, existing companies will no longer have to run so fast to keep up with technological change. As a result, there will be less demand for consulting firms to put in mammoth new information systems, and less need for hiring large numbers of newly minted MBAs and college grads each year.

The venture capital slump that accompanies the Internet Depression will also have a tremendous depressing effect on employment. In 1999, almost $50 billion in venture capital flowed into new startups, most of which likely ended up being spent within the first year. Given that $50 billion, a reasonable estimate would suggest that anywhere from 300,000 to 800,000 new jobs were generated by venture capital that year.[2] As the flow of VC drops off, many of those jobs will disappear.

The much-discussed shortage of IT workers could turn into a

surplus almost overnight. An April 2000 study from the Information Technology Association of America suggested that out of 1.6 million new IT jobs in 2000, half would go unfilled. But as the growth rate of the IT sector slackens, many of these unfilled openings will quickly evaporate.

Educated workers who have grown accustomed to never being out of a job will face a much tougher labor market. In May 2000, the unemployment rate for managers and professionals stood at 1.7%. A sustained tech downturn could easily send that rate soaring as high as 5%, or one out of twenty managers and professionals. That doesn't seem like much, but to people with big mortgages and college tuitions to pay, any sustained stretch of unemployment will be devastating.

The damage will be even more widespread. One of the remarkable features of the New Economy has been the rise of a whole class of freelancers and temporary workers. To function at peak efficiency, the high-risk, high-innovation New Economy requires a mobile attack force willing to take jobs at risky startups and accept stock options as a key part of their compensation. Indeed, the lack of workers willing to take such risks is one of the main reasons the New Economy has had trouble taking hold in Europe and Japan.

More generally, the rapid pace of innovation places a premium on flexibility in every part of the economy. Companies are much more willing to hire people during periods of rapid technological change if they know they can get rid of them quickly. Software and manufacturing firms, hospitals, retailers, and even government agencies are using temporary workers more extensively.

One indication: Employment at temporary help firms represented only 0.6% of the total nonfarm workforce in 1981, and 1.4% in 1990, at the beginning of the last two recessions. But as of early 2000, such employees of temp firms made up a much larger 2.7% of total jobs. And that number doesn't include independent contractors or temporary workers directly hired by companies who, according to the Bureau of Labor Statistics, make up at least another 6% of the workforce.[3]

The downside of flexibility is that companies have no reason to hold on to temporary workers when times turn bad. During a recession, employment at temporary help firms generally drops about four times as much as overall employment. In the recession of 1981–82, for example, overall employment fell by about 3%, but temporary employment fell by 12%. The 1974–75 and 1990–91 recessions showed roughly the same patterns. The recent proliferation of temporary workers means that unemployment could rise very quickly when the downturn hits.

THE FATE OF HOUSEHOLD PROSPERITY

After nearly a decade of economic expansion, many American households feel like they are in good shape. Certainly the past few years have been kind to consumers. Rising incomes helped fuel soaring spending. Although households kept borrowing, their financial assets—in particular, stocks—were rising even faster (see Table 7.1).

There are several reasons, however, for consumers to be

Table 7.1   The Economic Health of the American Consumer

	Percentage Change, 1995–1999[a]	Increase, 1995–1999[a] (trillions of dollars)
Disposable income	23%	1.3
Consumer spending	27%	1.4
Household debt	35%	1.7
Stock market wealth	115%	7.0
Net worth	52%	14.2

Sources: Bureau of Economic Analysis; Federal Reserve.

[a]Measured from the fourth quarter of 1995 to the fourth quarter of 1999.

extremely cautious about spending as the economy slows. First, as we saw in Chapter 5, both wage growth and stock market wealth are now closely tied to the rapid growth of the tech industry. Any tech slowdown will lead to a synchronized falloff in both wages and stock market wealth that will affect everyone, not just workers in the tech sector. When the tech boom slows, Americans will be hit by a double whammy—fewer dollars in their pockets and reduced financial assets.

Second, an increasing share of pay is "variable," coming in the form of bonuses, stock options, and other types of compensation that will go down when profits tail off. Finally, the enormous amount of debt Americans have taken on will become a much heavier burden as the economy slows.

As a result, consumers may find it necessary to cut their spending faster than in any recent downturn. This will come as a surprise to many Americans, who are used to reaching for their wallets even during slow times. In the Old Economy business cycle, consumer spending was one of the most stable parts of GDP. Wages didn't vary much over the business cycle, households could borrow to cover temporary losses of income, and the government safety net, in the form of Social Security, Medicare, unemployment insurance, and the like, provided a floor under income and spending for many Americans.

The government safety net is still in place, although somewhat tattered. All told, government spending, including Social Security, payrolls for the military, teachers, and police, and government purchases, equals about 25% of the economy. That's down from 31% in 1981, but still far higher than it was in 1929.

Nevertheless, household spending will come under increasing stress in the Internet Depression. First, the wealth of Americans—and therefore their spending—is increasingly tied to the stock market. According to the latest data from the Federal Reserve, equity shares as a share of financial assets rose from 19% in 1989 to 38% in 1999. That means any variability in the equity prices is transmitted to consumer spending. Like pulling on a rubber band, the response of consumers to a change in market wealth may not be immediate, but it will eventually come.

But the threat to household prosperity goes beyond that. To a growing extent, companies have used stock options and bonuses to reward workers, rather than boost base pay. This use of "variable pay" has risen sharply in recent years. According to a survey by Hewitt Associates, a benefits consulting firm, variable pay awards such as bonuses and stock options made up 9.6% of payroll costs for managers and professionals in larger companies in 2000, compared to only 6.4% in 1994 and 3.8% in 1991.[4]

The implication is that almost 10% of pay for the highest-paid corporate workers is poised to disappear if the economy turns down. Stock options will become worthless while bonuses evaporate. The effect will be the same as a massive across-the-board drop in wages, something that has not happened even in the deepest postwar recessions.

There is another factor: the high debt burden of many households. As expectations of future growth have risen, people have responded by borrowing more. The ratio of household debt to disposable income rose to 95% in 1999, up from 80% in 1989, the year that was the high point of the 1980s debt explosion (see Figure 7.1). To put that amount of additional debt in perspective, it's as if you had $100,000 in after-tax income, and you borrowed another $15,000.

In part, families took advantage of rising home prices to take out money to use for spending. Thus, the amount of equity that people have in their homes shrank, from 59.3% in 1993 to 55.5% in 2000. The data also suggest that people took on a lot of new debt to start businesses. The median debt level for self-employed workers skyrocketed from $44,000 in 1995 to $68,000 in 1998 in inflation-adjusted dollars, a 54% increase. By comparison, people who work for someone else have seen only a 15% increase in debt.

So far debt has not pinched households because interest rates have been comparatively low and income growth has been

Figure 7.1   The Debt Problem Grows Larger.
Sources: Federal Reserve Board; Bureau of Economic Analysis.
[a]First quarter.

strong. The share of household income going to debt service has been gradually rising and stood at 13.6% of disposable personal income in the first quarter of 2000. That's the highest level since 1987, but still below the 14.2% peak of the 1980s. Moreover, because debt has risen more slowly than the value of financial assets such as stocks and real estate, the net worth of households has risen substantially.

This can change quickly. Households have been adding debt during a period of prosperity, but what will happen if the economy starts to slow? In the early stage of the slide downward, consumers will likely keep spending, under the assumption that the dip is temporary. During this stretch, they will run up their credit cards in order to maintain their standard of living.

If the economy bounces back quickly, this extra debt is no

problem. Indeed, the willingness to keep spending through temporary slowdowns—"consumption smoothing" in economists' terms—reduces the volatility of growth.

But consumption smoothing becomes the wrong strategy if the rate of innovation slows and the economy starts to slip into depression. In that case, the correct course for consumers is to cut back their spending sharply in order to pay off their debt. People who do that will have a better chance of making it through the downturn in good shape.

Unfortunately, the strategy of reduced spending, while making sense for individuals, may hurt the broader economy. A similar cutback by debt-laden consumers helped steepen the initial plunge into depression in the 1930s, and the same thing could happen this time. This is part of what will hurt the U.S. economy on the downside of the tech cycle.

INVESTMENT BOOM, INVESTMENT BUST

For most corporations, the 1990s were a stressful period, as managers had to cope with new technologies and threats from new competitors. But as difficult as the boom was, the bust will be far worse. Corporate executives who have grown accustomed to rapid growth will be faced with a host of new problems.

When the downturn hits, the most important decision for corporations is whether to continue investing at current levels or to cut back. Big capital expenditures, especially on borrowed money, expose firms to a lot more risk in a weak economy. Nothing can produce bankruptcy faster than expanding and then discovering that the anticipated market has evaporated. On the other hand, that sort of bet can pay off big if the demand bounces back quickly: the companies that fared best in the 1980s and 1990s were those such as Intel that kept investing right through the downturns.

If this were an Old Economy business cycle, companies would cut back on capital spending as they adjusted to the slowdown, but not by very much. In the conventional business-school view, the decision to build a new factory or open a new store is determined by such mundane factors as the expected growth of the target market, the cost of the investment, and the prevailing interest rate (the cost of the money). And the truth is, these things don't change much over time. For example, during the last recession, at the beginning of the 1990s, capital spending by businesses, adjusted for inflation, dropped by only about 7% from its high at the beginning of 1990 to its low at the beginning of 1992. Considering that capital spending has more than doubled in the 1990s, that sort of drop would feel like a pinprick today.

But the New Economy tech cycle, in which innovation is neither slow nor constant, may create a sharper boom-and-bust pattern in business investment. It is important to remember that during the expansion phase of the tech cycle, which was accompanied by rapid technological progress, investment expanded far faster than forecasters had predicted, as the U.S. nearly matched the supposedly unbeatable Japanese investment splurge of the 1980s. Part of the reason for the underestimate of investment was that the cost of capital goods fell much more sharply than expected, making investment in labor-saving equipment like a bargain compared to paying for workers. From 1995 to 2000, the price of info tech equipment and software plunged by about 25%. Meanwhile, the cost to a business for an hour of worker time, including benefits, rose by about 20%. In addition, the breakthrough nature of the new technologies meant that companies had to invest simply to keep up with competitors, even if the investments didn't pay off immediately.

But when the tech cycle swings down and the rate of innovation slows, managers will have to reconsider the way they think about their investments. Instead of viewing their investments as a defense against potential competitors or an option on future innovations, companies will start to look at the value they provide right now. In the cold light of day, it will become more difficult to justify investments without a clear payoff. The "future factor" will evaporate when the rate of technological innovation slows. Nobody wants to pay a big entry fee for a game with a small prize.

As a result, the decline in business spending is likely to be much sharper than expected. Information technology and the Internet will still offer big benefits. But a business that has long invested heavily in information technology will not have to replace its computers every two years or so to keep up with the increase in speed and memory.

These considerations will weigh even more heavily on companies that have been borrowing extensively to pay for their capital expenditures. The debt of nonfinancial corporations rose by 34% between the beginning of 1997 and the beginning of 2000, adjusted for inflation, the biggest increase since the early 1980s.

If the Federal Reserve reacts to the downturn by cutting rates, won't that be a good reason for corporate executives to invest more? Historically, investment-driven booms have often been followed by equally deep busts. In Japan, corporate investment spending in 1999 was still about 25% below its peak of 1991, having failed to recover substantially even after the Bank of Japan cut interest rates to nearly zero. As economists at Goldman Sachs noted in early 2000:

> Such an investment boom and bust can take a very long time to play out, but the hangover tends to be substantially greater than after the normal business cycle. . . . If investment were to collapse as the boom ends, monetary policy would lose much of its power to support economic activity. The expected return on new investment would plummet faster than the ability of the monetary authorities to support it by easing monetary policy.[5]

NAVIGATING THE FINANCIAL STORM

One characteristic of the New Economy boom is that many more people than ever before have a substantial share of their savings invested in the stock market. Their future financial health depends on understanding how to play the coming tech downturn.

Or perhaps "play" is the wrong word. As the economy loses altitude, any asset linked to expectations of future growth will fall in value. From the stock market to the banks to the mortgage lenders, there will be no safe haven: The real question for investors will be which part of the financial system is going to break first, and which asset is going to fall farthest.

First to go, as I noted before, will be the New Economy stocks that have led the boom. Since the price of these stocks depended on assuming strong rates of future growth and innovation, the tech slowdown will hit them particularly hard. Tech and communications stocks will plunge as investors will flee from the New Economy stocks into the brick-and-mortar companies. That process may have started in the spring of 2000, when many of the Internet stocks collapsed. Such New Economy stalwarts as Amazon.com saw their prices plummet, as investors decided that they could not see how the companies could ever make money.

Particularly vulnerable are the telecom companies, which have been taking on massive amounts of debt to fund the expansion of capacity necessary to build the information infrastructure. In some sense they had no choice—it was either borrow and build, or get left behind. But these companies are used to being protected by regulators during downturns, and being guaranteed a decent rate of return on their investments. This time around, things will be different—it won't be pleasant. With mammoth debts taken on to fund expansion and much less protection from regulators, the telecom companies will find themselves squeezed for profit—and their stocks will fall accordingly.

Old Economy companies will temporarily be able to maintain their profit margins by shifting to cost-cutting rather than expansion of capacity as the main goal of their technology spending. Indeed, for a while it will seem like the revenge of the Old Economy. But as the overall economy slows and demand drops, Old

Economy companies, too, will see their profits fall. The carnage will spread across the entire market.

The other important factor will be company size. The small, innovative companies, cut off from financing, will burn through their money quickly. Without liquidity, they will either go under or be forced to dramatically curtail their R&D and product development efforts, the equivalent of slow suicide.

Big companies with massive cash cushions, on the other hand, will fare much better. In particular, Microsoft and Intel together had more than $30 billion in cash and short-term investments in 1999, equal to about 60% of their sales. Even if their profits plunge, they will be able to keep spending on new products, giving them a mammoth edge when things turn sour.

There is historical precedent for the advantages of size during a deep downturn. For most of the Great Depression, the largest companies were able to stay in the black, on average, while smaller rivals ran big losses. As a result, the larger companies took bigger and bigger shares of their markets. For example, most of the smaller automobile makers did not survive the Depression, leaving Ford, General Motors, and Chrysler with virtually the entire market.

THE DEBT CRISIS

Obviously, when faced with a steep market decline, many investors are tempted to retreat and move their money into bonds and money market funds. Will these investments be a safe haven from the storm?

It depends. Obviously the financial markets are sounder and more stable than they were in 1929. Virtually every aspect of the financial system is better controlled and better regulated. For example, federal insurance of all bank deposits below a certain size has virtually eliminated bank panics. The banks are well capitalized, and the supervision of the SEC and other regulatory bodies makes the financial system more transparent and prevents many problems before they occur.

Perhaps most important, the Federal Reserve has come to understand, as it did not in 1929 and the early 1930s, that it has a key role as the "lender of last resort" when the financial system seems about to become unhinged. In this role, the Fed quickly steps forward, as it did after the 1987 crash and the 1998 financial crisis, to reassure the markets that funds will be available for financial institutions if needed.

The implication is that in a short tech downturn, bonds and money market funds should be quite safe. Nevertheless, there are two caveats. First, as the economy slows and the rate of innovation drops off, there will be pressure on corporations to raise prices. If the Fed keeps interest rates high in response to this "suppressed" inflation, it could be the worst of all worlds for bonds—higher inflation and rising rates.

Moreover, the buildup of private-sector debt in recent years is a sword of Damocles hanging over investors that could drop if the Internet Depression gets bad enough. The key to understanding the potential debt crisis is to realize that banks—which are protected by deposit insurance—have become much less important for borrowing and lending. In the 1960s and 1970s, banks were able to raise money with low and no-interest savings and checking accounts, made attractive because the deposits were insured by the Federal Deposit Insurance Corporation, and then lend those funds out in the form of business loans, mortgages, and consumer installment debt.

Banks still make loans and issue credit cards. But instead of funding their lending out of their own resources, banks and other financial institutions are securitizing them—repackaging their loans and either selling them to another financial institution or as a package to investors. For mortgages and consumer credit, the impact of securitization is enormous. This is a real change in the way America finances its homes and businesses, and in many ways it is a positive one. Indirectly, it enables businesses and consumers to tap into the entire capital market, which gives them more access to cheaper credit. And because issuers can diversify, they are at less risk, and so can offer lower rates to more people.

Moreover, the combination of banks and capital markets provides two avenues through which credit can flow, making the financial system more resistant to problems. In the early 1990s, the U.S. went through a "credit crunch" in which many of the biggest banks, near insolvency from big real estate losses, had throttled back on lending. But the capital markets did not shut down. Indeed, corporations were able to keep raising money by issuing corporate bonds. On the other hand, in the fall of 1998, many of the global capital markets froze in the aftermath of Russia's default and the collapse of the hedge fund Long-Term Capital Management, but the banks were able to keep lending. The more money can pass back and forth between these two channels for lending, the less likely such freezes become.

But while securitization has enabled financial institutions to lend more freely, it has also made them much more dependent on the willingness of investors to absorb the debt. Banks no longer lend out the deposits that they have on hand—they have to get other people to invest in them. This system has never been stress-tested by the kind of deep downturn that would make investor capital dry up.

The biggest danger to the mortgage market would be a steep fall in the price of homes. Unfortunately, that seems highly likely if and when the Internet Depression arrives. Real estate prices have soared in the past few years, led by Silicon Valley, where the price of a home has skyrocketed beyond belief. The demand for these houses is being driven by the growth of precisely those industries that will be hit hardest by the Internet Depression. If prices collapse, it will become a lot harder to place mortgage securities, driving up mortgage rates, which will drive the home market down even farther.

In the worst-case scenario, we would start seeing defaults in money market mutual funds, which are presumed safe. A large portion of the return on money market funds comes from their holdings of mortgage securities and asset-backed securities tied to credit card debt. But if the economy slips deep enough, such securities will become quite risky.

CHAPTER EIGHT

Will the Internet
Depression Go Global?

DURING THE SECOND half of the 1990s, the U.S. was the prime mover for the global economy. While Japan stagnated, East Asia collapsed, and Europe slogged along, America ran up big trade deficits and soaked up whatever excess capacity the rest of the world had to offer. Indeed, the strong growth in the U.S. may have helped prevent a global depression in the aftermath of the 1997 East Asian financial crisis.

By early 2000, however, there were signs that an American-style New Economy was spreading to Europe and Asia, as formerly skeptical companies and policymakers began to embrace the idea of tech-driven growth. European companies such as Nokia and Ericsson established strong positions in key areas such as wireless technology. Japan began taking advantage of its traditional strength in consumer electronics, and Taiwan's semi-conductor foundries became critical suppliers for U.S. tech companies. Perhaps most important, a venture capital market started to slowly develop outside the U.S., although it remained young and small compared to the mammoth flows going through the venture funds of Silicon Valley, Boston, and elsewhere.

The question, then, is whether Europe and Asia can become

the motors for world growth if the U.S. stalls out. Certainly strong growth in the rest of the world, if it pans out, could boost U.S. exports and help mitigate any tech downturn. But it's not yet clear whether the global economy would be victim, villain, or savior in an American tech downturn. For one thing, the New Economy in Europe and Asia is in its early stages and may not provide enough thrust to keep the U.S. from crashing.

Remember also that the New Economy is not based just on technology but on new financial markets as well. In the 1990s the global financial system proved to be far less stable than economist's had hoped. When the U.S. economy slows, will the global markets stand up to the strain? The answer to this question could be crucial for determining whether the Internet Depression is relatively short, or deep, long, and painful.

THE MIXED NEWS

Until fairly recently, most European and Asian business leaders and politicians viewed the American New Economy with a mixture of disbelief and envy. Like many U.S. economists, they did not see how a U.S. economy that sputtered during the 1980s could be so quickly transformed into a dynamo. Europe and Japan had nothing like the U.S. venture capital markets and could not seem to match the rich flow of ideas and new companies coming out of Silicon Valley.

Now that may be changing. Most economic forecasters are calling for growth in Japan and Europe to accelerate over the next couple of years. For example, the June 2000 forecast from the OECD—the Paris-based organization of industrialized countries—predicted that Europe would grow at an annual rate over 3.2% in 2000 and 2001, faster than the 1.9% growth it averaged during the 1990s. Japan shows hesitant signs of pulling out of its slump.

And in Europe, at least, there are the beginnings of a venture capital sector able to fund small, innovative firms. In 1999, European venture capital firms invested 10.6 billion euros (roughly $11.3 billion) in startups and expansion funding. That's up about 80% from the previous year, although still far below the U.S. level. Such funding for small, innovative businesses is absolutely essential to support technological change and force existing businesses to adopt new technology faster. The latter may be even more important in Europe than in the U.S., given the dominance of large European companies that grew up under regulation and state control.

But it is still not clear that demand growth in Europe and Asia is going to be strong enough to keep the U.S. afloat. In Europe especially, the signs of a fast-growth, high-investment New Economy are much scarcer than people had hoped, despite the shift to a single currency across much of the continent. In 1999, productivity growth in the single currency region was an abysmal 0.8%, down from the 1.6% rate of the previous four years. Even assuming some error in measuring productivity, that's still pretty low. And there's no apparent investment boom in Europe either. Production of capital goods rose at only 2.1% in 1999, a very low number, and there's no concrete proof yet of a boom in European IT spending.

Nor is it clear that the global financial markets can absorb a depression or deep recession in the U.S. with equanimity. The U.S. stock markets are still the largest and most liquid in the world, the dollar is still the currency of choice for most international transactions, and most of the largest and most important global financial institutions are still based in the U.S.

THE VULNERABLE COUNTRY

Ironically, a resurgence in Europe and Asia could actually *trigger* a financial crisis in the U.S., and perhaps even globally. The New

Economy boom in the U.S. has relied on an expanding flow of money from overseas to finance investment and consumption at home. If the New Economy spreads and foreign investors suddenly decide that there are better opportunities in other parts of the world, the resulting shift in investment flows could do a great deal of damage to the U.S. economy.

The essence of the fluid global capital markets is that investors get to choose where they put their money—and the fact that they kept putting it into the U.S. in the 1990s was a key reason why the upside of the tech cycle went on so long. Between 1995 and 1999, foreign investors poured more than $2.8 trillion into buying U.S. financial and business assets. In effect, the flow of funds into the U.S. financed much of the investment boom of the 1990s. In 1995, foreign money was only 8% of total U.S. investment (residential and business). By the first quarter of 2000, foreign money had risen to 26% of total investment (see Figure 8.1). To get

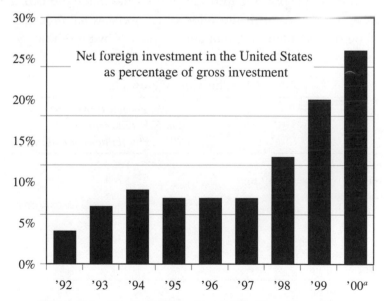

Figure 8.1   Foreign Money Funds The Investment Boom.
Source: Bureau of Economic Analysis.
[a]First quarter.

another sense of just how much the U.S. has come to depend on foreign investors, consider that in 1999 the flow of money from abroad was twice as big as all of household savings.

What made the U.S desirable as an investment destination during this period was its rapid innovation and productivity growth. The creation of new technologies and new financial markets, inextricably linked, opened up opportunities for high-return investments that existed nowhere else. And foreign companies also wanted to get a piece of the fast-growing U.S. economy by buying companies or building plants in the U.S. Foreign direct investment totaled over $700 billion between 1995 and 1999 (see Table 8.1).

Foreign investors have been major buyers of corporate bonds, stocks, and especially U.S. government securities, which looked like safe investments. Non-U.S. investors held 36% of U.S. Treasury debt at the beginning of 2000, up from 18% in 1993.

All this money pouring into the country has made the U.S. a massive net debtor, with the value of its overseas liabilities exceeding the estimated value of assets overseas by more than $1

Table 8.1   The Money Flows In

	Net Foreign Purchases of U.S. Financial Assets, 1995–1999 (billions of dollars)
Total	2808
Foreign direct investment in U.S. businesses	734
U.S. government securities	605
Corporate bonds	507
Other financial assets	460
Agency securities[a]	269
Corporate equities	233

Source: Federal Reserve.

[a]Primarily securities issued by such government-sponsored enterprises as Freddie Mac and Fannie Mae.

trillion at the end of 1999. It's important to realize, of course, that official figures on international capital flows are more guess-work than precise measurement. The flows are hard to track and subject to revision. Still, even if the $1 trillion figure is off, there is little doubt that the U.S. owes a large and steadily increasing amount of money.

In theory, a country that is a big international borrower will eventually pay a price, in two ways. First, it will find itself paying out interest on the investment. Assuming that the long-term return on capital is 10%, a $1 trillion debt means that we could expect to send roughly $100 billion a year overseas. Out of a $9 trillion economy, that's not much.

But there's a bigger problem: the U.S. risks a devastating run on its currency. Suppose the dollar slips against other major cur-rencies, such as the euro and the yen. Several aspects of the Internet Depression could cause such a slip, including a slow-down in growth or a rise in inflation. Investors who have money in the U.S. will see their investment become less valuable in their own currency, and if they expect the dollar to fall farther, they will want to pull out their investments before that happens.

But these investments are in dollars, and getting out of them puts more dollars on the market, pushing the currency down even farther and setting up a self-reinforcing negative cycle. In short order a net inward flow of funds can turn into a hemor-rhage. The result would be a plunging stock market, skyrocket-ing interest rates, soaring inflation, and a sharp slowdown in the economy.

This is the sort of run that devastated Mexico and the coun-tries of East Asia in the 1990s. To be sure, the U.S. is far less vul-nerable than any of these other countries to a currency panic. Unlike them, the U.S. is borrowing in its own currency, which means debt payments do not go up if the currency falls. Much of the money flowing into the country has gone into tangible invest-ments—factories and existing companies—which are difficult if not impossible to get out of quickly. The Daimler purchase of Chrysler will not be easily undone, no matter what happens to the dollar. In addition, the U.S. is perceived as a safe harbor for investments—the country least likely to suffer a coup, revolution, bankruptcy, or other upheaval. Finally, and very important, the Federal Reserve has enormous credibility. Everyone believes it will run a monetary policy that will not permit runaway inflation and deep devaluation of the dollar.

But the Fed may face a no-win choice if the economy heads into a tech downcycle. Cutting interest rates to boost the economy makes the dollar less attractive to foreign investors, and only accelerates the outflow of money. But the medicine that prevents devaluation and inflation—high interest rates—is precisely the policy that would prolong the downturn.

THE SECOND MISTAKE GOES GLOBAL

This potential bind has been on the mind of economists since the 1980s, when the U.S. first began running big trade deficits, and these worries have only intensified. In their 2000 book, *Global Finance at Risk*, economists John Eatwell and Lance Taylor warn that

> the potential disequilibria—portfolio shifts away from the U.S., bigger international obligations on its debt, and growing financial stress on the household sector—could begin to feed on one another and on the views of the markets. At that point . . . all hopes for global macro stability could disappear.[1]

The solution would be for all the major central banks to cut interest rates simultaneously. That would stimulate both the U.S. and global economies, without encouraging the further flow of money out of the U.S.

Unfortunately, it is not obvious that international cooperation would be forthcoming. The Great Depression was marked by a rolling deflation as country after country jacked up interest rates in order to staunch the outflow of gold. In each country, the central bank thought it was doing the right thing, and perhaps individually they were. But collectively, they brought on a collapse of the global economy.

Could such a scenario happen again? It's not likely. Yet a deep downturn in the U.S. is just the kind of event that could set off a rolling financial panic. A problem in one country makes it more likely that investors will look for—and find—similar problems in other countries. In country after country, stock markets could plummet, debt markets could freeze up, and central banks could be forced to raise rates to prevent a currency collapse.

This sort of contagion is one of the most devastating features of any financial crisis. Panic is transmitted across national boundaries far faster than any changes in the underlying economy. The collapse of the Mexican peso in 1994 and 1995, for example, led investors to pull their money out of other Latin American currencies, fearing a similar crisis would hit those countries as well.

Open global capital markets increase the chances of contagion. Note Eatwell and Taylor:

> In the past, the main strategy against contagion was compartmentalization and segmentation of markets. . . . Following the breakdown of barriers between financial markets . . . all segments of the system are now tightly interdependent, both nationally and internationally.[2]

But nobody knows how the major central banks might react to a rolling financial panic, since they are trying to follow two separate and diametrically opposed policy rules. On the one hand, it has been drummed into the heads of central bankers since the 1930s that the appropriate reaction to a financial crisis is to lower rates and flood the markets with liquidity, at least temporarily. On the other hand, faced with an outflow of money from a country, central banks are impelled to raise rates to convince foreign investors that they shouldn't pull their money out. Paul Krugman observes that

> following an economic policy that makes sense in terms of the fundamentals is not enough to assure market confidence. In fact, the need to win that confidence can actually prevent a country from following otherwise sensible policies. . . . The overriding objective of policy must therefore be to mollify market sentiment.[3]

The corollary is that it has become much tougher for most countries to run expansionary monetary policies. Because it is so easy to move money across borders, cutting interest rates and pumping money into an economy may not provide much stimulus. Instead, the money may flow out of the country, doing nothing more than driving down the exchange rate and driving up the price of imported goods.

In addition, the conventional wisdom among economists in recent years has been that the best macroeconomic policy involves fiscal austerity, balanced budgets, limited social spending, and a tight monetary policy to keep inflation down. This advice is regularly offered by the International Monetary Fund (IMF) to virtually every country it lends money to. Similarly, for many years the economists at the OECD have been calling for the U.S. to boost interest rates in order to prevent inflation. And the fact that most influential economists around the world have been trained at major Western universities goes a long way toward maintaining this policy consensus. Thomas Palley, chief economist at the AFL-CIO, writes: "Since economists act as policy advisers around the world, the economics profession has become a de facto means for coordinating and implementing deflationary policy on a global scale."[4]

Faced with the need to run an expansionary monetary policy

in order to head off a financial crisis, three major central banks—the European Central Bank (ECB), the Bank of England, and the Bank of Japan—might hesitate. In particular, the founding charter of the ECB assigns it the single task of fighting inflation (the Federal Reserve, by contrast, has the joint goals of low inflation and low unemployment). Thus the ECB was willing to raise interest rates in the spring of 2000, even though prices were rising at less than 2%, for fear that inflation would accelerate sometime in the future. In testimony before the European Parliament in June 2000, Willem Duisenberg, the president of the ECB, said,

> Our main mandate is to preserve price stability. . . . We look at the figures about 1½ years from now . . . what we expect them to be at that time in our forward-looking assessment. . . . We still have to build up our track record of credibility and confidence, and that will take time.[5]

Unfortunately, time is in short supply in a crisis.

THE MISSING INSTITUTION

One of the most important consequences of the Great Depression in the U.S. was that the Federal Reserve acknowledged and accepted its role as "lender of last resort" for the U.S. financial system. In the absence of a lender of last resort, financial institutions and financial markets are subject to snowballing panic runs by frightened investors. Once the panic gets going, investors and lenders cannot risk being left with nothing if everyone else has pulled out first. As a result, there's a stampede for the door in which previously sound financial institutions may be crunched out of existence. This problem only gets worse with more sophisticated financial markets—the easier it is to move money around, the more exposed the markets are to panic attacks.

The solution is a lender of last resort—a central bank standing ready to lend virtually without limit to any financial institution that is solvent but squeezed by a financial panic. To put it a different way, the central bank can print money in any quantity and temporarily lend it to stressed financial institutions to satisfy their obligations. That calms the fears of investors who worry about being the last ones out the door, and keeps financial panics from spiraling out of control. As Kindleberger puts it, "The role of the lender of last resort is to provide the public good of stability."[6]

On a national level, the lender of last resort concept can work well, especially when a country is blessed with a central bank with the credibility of the Federal Reserve and a central bank chairman as respected as Alan Greenspan. Investors in such a country may correctly assume that the central bank will step in to clean up any problem that gets big enough to threaten the financial system, and that makes them far less fearful of losing their money. The result is a far more efficient and stable system.

But there is no lender of last resort for the whole world, and this missing institution poses one of the most serious threats to the global economy. The international financial system has been hit by almost yearly crises, from the failure of the European monetary system in 1992, to the collapse of the Mexican peso in 1994 and 1995, to the East Asian debacle in 1997, to the Russian default and the near-bankruptcy of Long-Term Capital Management in 1998. As long as there is no global lender of last resort, the crises will surely continue.

The problem, of course, is that there is no global government to empower a central bank to serve as a stabilizing influence. International economists and policymakers have spent the past few years trying unsuccessfully to paste together a substitute.

One possible substitute is the International Monetary Fund. For smaller countries, the IMF can pass as an ersatz lender of last resort, but it simply does not have enough money to deal with a crisis in an even medium-sized industrial economy such as South Korea's. As of the spring of 2000, the IMF formally could draw on resources equivalent to $300 billion. But only about $60 billion of that could be tapped quickly, an insignificant sum compared to the foreign liabilities of a country the size of South Korea.

The other difficulty with the IMF is that it imposes conditions on the economic policy of borrowers, such as budget cutbacks, before it pays out the loans. From the perspective of influencing economic policy, this is probably the right thing to do. But conditional loans are not as effective in putting out financial panics, since negotiating them takes time, which is at a premium when the bottom is falling out of financial markets. "Liquidity with conditions," write Eatwell and Taylor, "is not liquidity."[7]

The other possibility is the Federal Reserve, which is already the central bank for almost one-third of the world's economy. Under certain circumstances in the past, the Fed has been able to act as a sort of international lender of last resort. Most recently, the Fed's three interest rate cuts in fall 1998 were an attempt to soothe traumatized global markets.

But the Fed can take on this role only in a limited sense. It is very tough for any central bank, even one as powerful as the Fed, to be active outside its jurisdiction. A lender of last resort must have regulatory control over the institutions to which it provides money, and must be able to close down institutions that are actually insolvent. Without that control—which is impossible when the financial markets and institutions are in other countries—a lender of last resort will find itself taken advantage of and abused.

The other problem, and perhaps a bigger one, is that the Fed cannot effectively act as a lender of last resort if the crisis takes the form of a flight from dollars. In that case the ability to print dollars won't do any good, since international investors won't want them. Pumping money into the system would only devalue the currency further, hastening the exodus. Rather than stimulate the economy, it would make imports more expensive and aggravate inflation.

Such a global financial crisis, once ignited by the tech downturn in the U.S., will become hard to control. Far better that U.S. policymakers take steps to stop the downturn before it goes too far—and those solutions will have to come from within.

CHAPTER NINE

Escape from the Internet Depression

This depression is more than a passing circumstance in our history; it is a crucial turning point in industrial civilization, not only for the United States, but for the world.[1]

—*Business Week*, October 29, 1930

THE LEGITIMACY OF capitalism is presently unchallenged. There is no credible competing economic system. Socialism and communism are effectively dead, and the Japanese model no longer holds the allure it did in the 1980s.

But after the boom, the New Economy will face its own difficult challenges. As the economy slows and goes into reverse, Americans will become less willing to accept the volatility and insecurity associated with innovation, financial markets, and global trade. As unemployment rises and incomes fall, there will be a monumental backlash.

What we will need is a 21st-century version of the Keynesian compact that ended the Great Depression. The broad outlines of the policy prescription are fairly clear: fiscal and monetary policies that support demand in the short run; an extended safety net that provides more security without eliminating market incentives;

long-run support for innovation; and more supervision and regulation of financial markets, both domestic and international.

But finding a route out of the Internet Depression that preserves the vigor of the New Economy will not be easy. The devil is in the details. It's going to be hard to come up with a set of policies that make economic sense and can also attract enough political support. One of the most pernicious effects of the Internet Depression will be to erode the political consensus in favor of the New Economy. The political landscape will look more like a shattered windshield: New Economy industry versus Old Economy industry, New Economy worker versus New Economy business, aging retiree versus young worker, large firm versus small firm, industrial countries versus the third world. It will be difficult to assemble a political coalition to support the actions needed to get back to rapid future growth.

Nevertheless, there will be a big payoff for finding the middle ground amid the political chaos. Just as the New Deal gave the Democrats a tremendous political edge, whichever party finds the right balance—between enough government intervention to stabilize the economy, but not so much as to lose the advantages of the market—will dominate politics for years to come.

THE POLITICS OF THE GOOD TIMES

A boom produces fuzzy politics. The trade-off between security and growth seems to disappear, and investors, workers, and businesses all celebrate open markets and risk-taking. During a boom, people don't want the government to do anything that might bring the good times to a halt.

The present favorable views of the New Economy are nourished by a prosperity that has touched almost everyone. For example, the real hourly wage for production and nonsupervisory workers—roughly the bottom three-quarters of the labor force—has risen every quarter since the New Economy began in the middle of 1995. That's after seventeen years of almost uninterrupted declines in real wages. The distribution of stock gains has also broadened, giving more Americans a stake in the New Economy no matter which industry they work in. As of 1998, 49% of families owned stock, either directly or through mutual funds and retirement accounts—up from 32% in 1989. Strikingly, stock ownership has even increased for poor families, with nearly one-quarter of families with incomes between $10,000 and $25,000 invested in the stock market.

The tight labor markets have cushioned the impact of rapid innovation and global competition. Even during the boom years, U.S. corporations repeatedly announced job cuts as they streamlined, reorganized, and otherwise adapted to the New Economy. Moreover, the number of manufacturing jobs fell by 400,000 between the middle of 1998 and the middle of 2000, even while imports have soared. Yet the unemployment rate has fallen almost continuously, even among groups that are typically left behind by good times. In particular, the black unemployment rate dropped from an average of 14.2% for 1992 to 7.7% for the first half of 2000.

The good times have made the policy differences between the parties less important. When Americans were asked who should get credit for the economy going well, the answer was neither the Democrats nor the Republicans. Rather, the hands-down winner was the technology industry, which was picked by 26% of respondents.[2]

The situation is similar to the political narrowing of the 1920s. In the 1928 presidential campaign, the Republican candidate, Herbert Hoover, ran on a platform of eliminating poverty. His campaign slogan was "A chicken in every pot and a car in every garage," and he proclaimed that Americans were "in sight of the day when poverty will be banished from this nation." His Democratic opponent, Alfred Smith, embraced the business community, and appointed as chairman of the Democratic National Committee John Raskob, chairman of General Motors' finance committee and a longtime Republican.

But the apparent consensus did not survive past 1929. In the same way, when the U.S. starts sliding into the downside of the tech cycle, consensus will be replaced by conflict.

THE DANGER OF GOING BACKWARDS

The Internet Depression could do grave damage to the forces that helped drive the New Economy. That doesn't mean technology is going to disappear: the knowledge of how to make microprocessors, splice fiber-optic cables, and write sophisticated software programs will not be lost any time soon. The Internet has become an integral part of the way companies do business. But the openness and the competition that fuel the New Economy could be in danger.

Free trade and open financial markets, which create the incentives for risk-taking and innovation, require political support, but under the stress of a deep downturn that support can erode. In an illuminating paper on the history of markets, Raghuram Rajan and Luigi Zingales warn that "we should be cautious against taking for granted that financial development is unidirectional, and that the current generalized consensus in favor of markets is irreversible . . . in time of crises a political backlash against markets may occur, which may have very long-term consequences."[3]

Several things happen as the economy slows. First, as the unemployment rate goes up, the potential losses to workers from trade and innovation get bigger. When the unemployment rate is around 4%, as it was in early 2000, then anyone who loses a job because of imports or technological change can easily find a new one. The fear of job loss, while never gone completely, is muted.

But as unemployment rises, workers must worry not about

switching to a different job but about the possibility of having no job at all. Rapid innovation and free trade become far more threatening, and call forth a much stronger political reaction. As Paul Krugman notes, "in a world where there is often not enough demand to go around, the case for free markets is a hard case to make."[4]

The widespread support for the stock market could ebb as well. Americans have much more of their wealth in equities than ever before, making them more vulnerable to market fluctuations. As the market plummets and losses mount, they will exert enormous political pressure to increase oversight of mutual funds and brokerage firms. Moreover, if pension funds lose large sums of money in their investments in venture capital and technology stocks, there will be strong demand to regulate those investments as well.

And the potential for a backlash against free trade is always lurking in the background. While we're not likely to return to the trade wars of the late 1920s and early 1930s, Americans have always been quite conflicted about trade. Polls show widespread support for free trade in principle, but when a poll question links increased imports to the possibility of lost jobs, Americans generally become more skeptical about trade.

The same ambivalence shows up at the corporate level. Technological change and free trade offer both new opportunities and new competitors. But it's far easier for companies to see the benefits of technology and trade when growth is strong. When growth weakens, the case for markets no longer looks so compelling.

As the depression spreads to other countries, it will undermine their incentive to participate in the global economy as well. Right now the plusses of opening up markets more than outweigh the minuses for most countries. Governments that are hostile to growth are shunned by foreign investors. But once the global economy cools, this threat will no longer be as effective, and parochial political concerns will come to the fore.

LINES OF CONFLICT

Given the ambivalence even in good times about technology, competition, the stock market, and free trade, the political consensus needed to stem the Internet Depression will be difficult to muster. Just when it is necessary to act quickly, support for any decisive action will become ever harder to obtain. On one level, the political landscape will be split between those who believe in minimal government intervention and those who believe that government needs to take a more active role in fighting the depression and protecting people from risk.

But it won't be a simple two-sided debate. Instead, it will be the political equivalent of a financial panic, where everyone tries to protect her or his own interests first. Conflicts papered over in good times will burst into view. Issues that had faded into the background—monetary policy, government intervention in the economy, support for R&D, control of financial markets, budget deficits, free trade, health care, the minimum wage—will once again become contentious.

Here are some of the fault lines:

Old Economy versus New Economy Industries

This is perhaps the critical political fight of the Internet Depression, because it will determine how aggressively monetary and fiscal policy are used to fight the downturn. During the good years, both New and Old Economy industries favored faster growth. That's why the National Association of Manufacturers, mostly representing the old-line companies, regularly called for lower interest rates in the 1990s.

But after the downturn hits, their interests will diverge. New Economy industries such as software and telecom, hit hard by the Internet Depression, will need as much growth as possible because they have made big upfront investments in developing new programs, building expensive telecom networks, and the like. They will unabashedly urge the government to get the economy expanding again by any means necessary. That will include both cutting rates and increasing government spending on higher education and R&D, even if the consequences include inflation and a budget deficit.

Old Economy industries like growth too. But because their markets don't have as much potential to expand quickly, they must focus on keeping costs under control. That means they would prefer much less inflation and higher levels of unemployment, which keeps wages down. Moreover, higher unemployment gives them a better chance of competing for workers with New Economy companies that can afford to pay a lot more.

New Economy Workers versus New Economy Firms

An essential part of the innovative thrust of the U.S. economy has been a skilled and mobile workforce that could move from company to company. This arrangement satisfied both employers and employees: companies could easily change their staffing as they went into new markets or adopted new products. Meanwhile, many of these short-timers, consultants, freelance workers, and contract workers were paid well and had the freedom to pick their work.

But when the downturn comes and the New Economy firms start exercising their option to let people go, workers will inevitably want more security and better safety nets. Such measures could be a win-win proposition for both workers and companies. On the one hand, they obviously benefit workers. At the same time, however, better safety nets also make it easier for new companies to obtain good workers, since workers would be more willing to leave their jobs and go where the growth is, making the labor market more flexible and thus increasing the prospects for growth. But there will be a tremendous dispute about who will pay for the increased security.

Big versus Small Companies

The boom of the 1990s treated both big and small companies well. Big companies saw their stock prices soar even as a gargantuan merger and acquisition wave made them bigger than ever. Small companies, meanwhile, had unprecedented access to the capital markets, enabling the successful ones to expand rapidly.

Big companies will suffer relatively less in the Internet Depression, especially when it comes to raising money. Even during tough times, big companies generally don't have trouble getting the capital they need. They can finance their R&D themselves and raise enough money for capital investments, and they have plenty of fat to cut if needed.

Smaller companies, however, often do not have the resources to survive a long dry spell. It becomes very hard for them to get the capital they need to survive. The credit crunch of the early 1990s, for example, hit small firms much harder than big businesses. Moreover, because small companies are generally less global than larger businesses, a U.S.-centered Internet Depression will hurt them more.

The consequence is that small businesses will push much harder than big ones for monetary and fiscal stimulus. They will want the Fed to pump liquidity into the economy even if doing so triggers inflation. But unlike workers, who will also favor liquidity, small companies will fight hard against any safety net that involves increased regulation and taxes. And they will favor loosening the regulations on financial markets rather than tightening them.

Old versus Young

It was widely anticipated that the 1990s would be a decade of generational wars, but the strong economy took care of all that. As growth accelerated, the date on which the Social Security Trust Fund was to run out of money moved ever farther away. Retirees enjoyed their stock market gains while the young cashed in the options they collected while working at hot startups.

Once things turn down, the generational struggle will reerupt with a vengeance. Older Americans—retirees and workers nearing retirement age—are sure to be primarily concerned with preserving their capital. That means they would be happy with a slow-growth, high-interest rate economic policy that kept their interest income high and reduced the risk of big losses. The young, by contrast, will favor an economic policy that maximizes long-term growth and innovation, even if it carries more risks. That puts them in the same camp as the New Economy industries.

The swing group will be the baby boomers. They intend to enjoy many years of retirement, which means that they need the economy to keep growing in order to provide the lifestyle they want. On the other hand, the closer they get to leaving the work-force, the more emphasis they will put on stability and security in their jobs and their investments. The political payoff will come for anyone who can convince the baby boomers that their retirement is safe, while keeping their support for innovation and free trade.

Nationalists versus Globalists

Perhaps the nastiest fight will be over the global economy. On one side will be the nationalists, in the U.S. and elsewhere, who don't want to give up any sovereignty. On the other side are the globalists, who favor a gradual extension of the power of international economic institutions as a way of opening up markets and damping down volatility.

In recent years, the passage of North American Free Trade Agreement (NAFTA) and the General Agreement on Tariffs and Trade (GATT), the admission of China to the World Trade Organization, and the creation of the European single currency are all signs that the globalists have slowly been gaining ground. But it is easy to be in favor of globalization in good times. The real test of global commitment to open markets and international cooperation will come during the Internet Depression.

FINDING THE MIDDLE GROUND

The essence of Keynesian thinking in the 1930s was the assertion that it was possible to reduce risk and volatility and provide some measure of insurance without really diminishing the central role of markets. That meant a program which combined government spending programs to boost demand, an immediate increase in monetary stimulus, safety-net programs such as Social Security, and increased regulation and supervision of financial markets. These measures left the basic market framework of the economy intact, while providing Americans with the assurance that the disaster of the Great Depression could not happen again. As Krugman notes:

> At a time when many of the world's intellectuals were convinced that capitalism was a failed system, that only by moving to a centrally planned economy could the West emerge from the great depression, Keynes was saying that capitalism was *not* doomed, that a very limited sort of intervention . . . was all that was needed to make the system work.[5]

The appropriate policy response to the Internet Depression would also try to strike a similar balance, providing some stability to the economy without destroying the benefits of markets. But because the New Economy is different than the Old Economy, the package of policies needed to counteract the downturn will also be different. For the New Economy, such a solution would have several different components:

Breaking the Downward Spiral

First it's essential that government support demand to stop the economy from going into a downward spiral (or bring it out of one). This support makes workers and companies more willing to take risks and supplies more incentives for innovation.

As economists Barry Bluestone and Bennett Harrison observe in their book, *Growing Prosperity,*

> Without the expectation of growth, innovation will be slow to evolve. Low expectations become a self-fulfilling prophecy. . . . Only with the anticipation of sufficient sales of new goods and

services is there adequate incentive for private sector innovation and investment to take place at levels sufficient to maintain faster growth.[6]

There is a consensus that the most effective antidote for a demand shortfall is to pump money into the economy. Studies have shown that monetary stimulus was far more important for ending the Great Depression than the New Deal's spending programs. Nevertheless, the decision about how much stimulus to use is likely to be surprisingly contentious, even after the economy slides into depression, because it will require accepting the risk of increased inflation. If history is any guide, there will be a substantial group of economists opposed to doing anything that might lift inflation, even if the economy is in a deep slump.

Similarly, it will be easy to agree that some form of fiscal stimulus is needed. But the nature of the stimulus will be at issue. On one side will be those who want to cut taxes. In particular, there will be a strong sentiment to reduce the capital gains tax. On the other side will be those who favor a more traditional liberal approach to fiscal stimulus. Bluestone and Harrison write:

> the government has a positive, activist role to play in stimulating aggregate demand. It can do this by encouraging wage growth through stronger trade unions, regular increases in the minimum wage, and deliberate antipoverty programs. Spending more on education, highways, and health care can help as well.[7]

There will be tremendous political support for such spending measures when the economy lags. In the end, it will be necessary to both cut taxes and boost spending.

Funding for Innovation.

Over the past ten years, the government has taken a steadily smaller role in the innovative process. Cutbacks in defense R&D and continued pressure to reduce the federal budget deficit have sharply reduced the supply of government R&D funds. In real terms, government R&D money peaked in 1987 and has fallen by almost 20% since. All told, the government share of R&D funding has fallen from 57% in 1970 to only 27% in 1999.

That isn't necessarily a bad thing—private funds for applied research and development are typically more productive than government funds. But the increased dependence on private funds makes R&D and innovative activity much more vulnerable to the ups and downs of the economy.

As the economy slips into a tech downturn, the government will need to run a countercyclical innovation policy in addition to a countercyclical fiscal policy. That means boosting government spending on R&D and innovation to make up part of the decline in private support. Part of the additional funding should be in basic research, but some should be for potentially commercial projects as well. Without such support the sophisticated agglomeration of technological skills and knowledge that has sustained the New Economy may gradually drift away.

This will involve much more government participation in Silicon Valley than the high-tech industry is comfortable with. But as sales fall, so will the industry's resistance to government money.

Another part of a countercyclical innovation policy will be more support for higher education of scientists and engineers. When innovation is slowing and technical people are losing their jobs, students will be discouraged from going into science, engineering, and computer-related areas. At that point government must lean against the tide and provide additional incentives to entice students to get natural science, computer science, and engineering degrees.

Paul Romer, a leading economic expert on innovation, has suggested providing training grants to undergraduate institutions for students receiving natural science and engineering degrees, as a way to increase the supply of workers with technical training. For the longer term, Romer has also suggested creating and funding a new class of portable graduate fellowships in natural science and engineering, not tied to any particular program. That would solve one of the biggest problems, which is a mismatch between the skills graduate students learn and the ones that employers need.[8]

Individual Security

Providing a stronger safety net for individuals is essential to maintaining political support for a high-innovation, high-growth economy. Otherwise people feel adrift and helpless when the ground moves under them. As Rajan and Zingales note,

> the competitive forces unleashed by the markets can destroy some forms of insurance provided by social and economic institutions. As a result, economic downturns can lead to a popular appeal from the masses for political action to reverse the effects of the market.[9]

There are several ways to broaden the safety net, including better unemployment insurance benefits, more portable pensions, and strengthening Social Security. But perhaps the most important change that needs to be made is to broaden health insurance and make it accessible to more people. This is especially important for the New Economy's contingent workforce—temporary workers, independent contractors, and the like. Only about 60% of contingent workers were covered by health insurance in 1999, according to the Bureau of Labor Statistics, compared to about 82% of workers with traditional jobs. Among temporary help agency workers, only 41% were covered by health insurance.

But the question of who will pay for broader health insurance, and how it will be organized, is already a matter of great dispute. Will it be companies, the workers, or government? How much choice will people have, and where will the financial incentives lie? Eventually some kind of health insurance legislation will pass—but the process will be long and agonizing.

Supervision and Regulation of Financial Markets

In the aftermath of the Great Depression, the federal government created the Securities Exchange Commission as well as a whole regulatory framework for the financial industry. While it may be necessary to fine-tune the regulation of domestic financial markets, the real need for increased supervision is in the international financial markets.

Unfortunately, for all the talk of a new financial architecture in the aftermath of the 1997 economic crisis in Asia, little has happened. Observes Stephen Roach, chief economist at Morgan Stanley Dean Witter,

> Despite the heightened incidence of crises and the increased integration of ever-faster-moving world financial markets, there is no global policy agenda. Policymakers remain largely dominated by domestic concerns. . . . Talk of reforming the architecture of the international financial system has lost momentum.[10]

E. Gerald Corrigan, former head of the Federal Reserve Bank of New York, warned in a May 2000 speech that "when the next major sovereign financial crisis occurs, we may find ourselves facing a situation in which both official and private creditors have been backed into a corner that leaves little maneuvering room."[11]

What's needed is a strengthening of the institutions for monitoring and regulating the global financial system in normal times, and for intervening more directly in times of crisis. The changes could take the form of international financial standards; or an explicit and binding cooperation agreement among the major central banks; or beefing up the International Monetary Fund into something closer to a global lender of last resort.

But all these measures require that countries, including the

U.S., give up some sovereignty and control. That will not happen until the Internet Depression has caused so much pain that nations are willing to pay the cost for stability.

THE NEW COALITION

Today's political parties are still trying to understand what Americans really need in the New Economy, even while they haven't fully absorbed the notion that the New Economy really exists. Politicians attribute the United States's current success in equal parts to the Internet, Alan Greenspan, and their own sagacity, and meanwhile keep promising more and more, like modern-day Herbert Hoovers offering two chickens in every pot. They mouth the words about providing security to workers to take risks, but concrete action is lacking. And that's not a surprise—with the economy booming, there is little political support for major changes.

That will change once the economy starts slipping. It may take time, but eventually a new coalition will emerge in support of the policies needed to keep the New Economy going. And eventually new politicians better able to understand the balance between security and growth that the New Economy demands, will arise as well. But it will be a long, slow battle. The policies that bring us out of the Internet Depression are likely to be only the beginning of a major political realignment that will take us well into the 21st century.

CHAPTER TEN

Regaining Our Faith in the Future

THIS HAS BEEN, in many ways, a forbiddingly pessimistic book, especially coming from a longtime optimist. At a time of blue skies, I have suggested that the structure of prosperity Americans have built over the past decade may soon be threatened by an economic storm of historic proportions. The misery and suffering that follow—especially in contrast with today's ease—will touch Wall Street, Silicon Valley, Main Street, and all points in between.

That damage will be very real—but the key question is whether short-term pain will lead to long-term stagnation. Some New Economy skeptics, relatively quiet during the past couple years of growth, will seize on the downturn as proof that the information revolution was overrated and the productivity gains of the 1990s were illusory. They will once again proclaim the basic mediocrity of the American economy and urge us to reduce our expectations.

But this advice will show a profound misunderstanding of where the true dangers lie. The New Economy is not simply higher productivity and rising incomes. Nor is it faster computers, bigger homes and cars, or even an all-pervasive Internet. The soul of the New Economy is the ability and willingness to take bigger risks, on individual and societal levels, in pursuit of growth, innovation, and change—and it's this willingness to take risks that will be tested by the coming downturn.

RISK AND GROWTH

The risk-taking institutions underlying the New Economy, if they can be maintained through the coming downturn, offer tremendous potential for long-term growth. Economic growth is usually associated with the simple idea of a bigger pie. But there is another aspect to growth, which rarely gets as much notice—the ability to take bigger risks. As a society gets richer, it can choose to devote more resources to exploration and experimentation, even if the odds of any particular venture's success are small. Rather than simply staying in the valley, scouting parties can be sent out to cross the river and go over the mountains. Poor societies, by contrast, cannot afford to take any unnecessary risks.

This difference between rich and poor countries is analogous to the different investment behavior of poor and rich individuals. A wealthy person can set aside enough money for a nice lifestyle and a financial cushion while putting the rest into lucrative investments like venture capital, hedge funds, and high-return stocks. Poor people, on the other hand, have no financial cushion and so have to choose lower-risk investments such as bank accounts.

From this perspective, the New Economy is a way of leveraging America's great wealth in pursuit of technological change and faster growth. The system of risk capital can create a multitude of new ventures, each of which has a high chance of failing, but which together create an environment of rapid growth and innovation.

This organized risk-taking, if it continues, could lay the foundation for a broad wave of innovation that could rival that of the early 20th century. Much of that innovation, of course, comes from the ongoing thrust of information technology, which has reinvigorated the economy. But there's much more. Attracted by the outsize returns on IT investments, investors have pumped billions of dollars into venture capital funds in the past couple of years. These giant pools of risk capital are now available for a wide range of innovative projects in fields other than information technology.

It is this next wave of innovations that are the future of the New Economy. Which industries will benefit from the availability of risk capital? Obviously biotechnology, which has already been one of the main recipients in the past decade, will continue to receive immense amounts of money. With the mapping of the human genome, there are more and more potential applications of biotech to medicine. And with the pools of available capital getting larger and larger, there is no reason why many of these applications cannot be explored simultaneously.

Venture capital will seek out other potential areas of innovation. For example, the ongoing deregulation of the electric and gas industries creates new opportunities to make money in energy-related startups. Venture funding is already financing the development and commercialization of such new energy technologies as microturbines and fuel cells. These and other new ways of generating, distributing, and using energy will be critical to the future of the New Economy, just as the energy-based innovations of the late 1800s, electricity and the internal combustion engine, were key to a century of growth.[1]

Then there is the use of space travel for profit-making ventures. With the exception of communication satellites, space-related activity has been primarily funded by governments, more concerned with national security and basic research than with any potential profits. But as the available pools of risk capital get larger and larger, they create more opportunities for the private sector to jump-start the commercialization of space in ways yet undreamed of.

And there's much more. As the reach of venture capital broadens, it will become easier to find funding for technologies that are now only in the earliest stages, such as nanotechnology—the construction and manipulation of micromachines. Economic growth will be boosted by not just one wave of innovation, but many, coming one after another. The willingness to make high-risk, high-return investments will sustain a long stretch of growth.

RISK AND RETURN

Getting to this rosy future won't be easy. When things start going wrong and the boom shifts to bust, optimism will give way to pessimism. Risks that once seemed perfectly natural will look totally unreasonable. Investors, workers, and businesses will all pull back from future-oriented investments because they will have lost faith that the future will be better.

If the tech slump turns into a depression, taking chances will become even harder. Americans will put their money into bank accounts rather than high-risk, high-growth stocks. They will not try to find new jobs in which they can be happier and more productive, because they will fear losing their current benefits. They will be scared to borrow to get an education because they will not know if they will have the resources to pay back a loan. Worst of all, they will turn down chances to work for startup companies because they crave the security that an established company brings. Notes one economist, "pessimism can cause people to live for today . . . to grab what they can without regard for others or for future consequences."[2]

The good news is that with the right policies, even a deep depression need not cripple America's economic future. Consider the first half of the 20th century, a fifty-year stretch that included the Great Depression and eleven recessions, some quite nasty in their own right. Wide swings in the economy were common. By the reckoning of the National Bureau of Economic Research, the U.S. spent fully 36% of that fifty-year stretch in recession or depression. Uncertainty and deprivation marked entire generations.

But the U.S. economy kept going despite the damage. This same fifty-year stretch was also one of the most impressive periods of technological progress the world had yet seen. From electricity to automobiles, telephones to radios to antibiotics, new technologies changed every aspect of home and work. Living standards soared for poor and rich alike, with average real per capita income more than doubling from 1900 to 1950. Life expectancy at birth increased from 47 to 68 years. This effectively doubled the length of working lifetimes, making it possible for people to get more education and still have time to make a contribution to society.

To match this record of achievement in the 21st century will require new policies and new politics that take into account the realities of the New Economy. Old policies, designed for the Old Economy, will only prolong the slump and delay the revival of support for innovation. Our obligation to our children is to take risks, to push out the boundaries, and when things break down to pick them up again and keep going. The most dangerous thing we could do would be to deny our wealth and become misers trying to hoard what we have. The only way through the Internet Depression is forward and faster. You can't slow a plane down to the speed of a car. What stops, dies. What grows, survives.

Notes

PREFACE

1. Michael Mandel, "The New Economy: For Better Or Worse," *Business Week*, October 19, 1998, p. 42.

CHAPTER ONE

1. Thomas Petzinger Jr., "So Long, Supply and Demand," *Wall Street Journal*, December 31, 1999, p. R31.
2. Charles Kindleberger, *The World in Depression, 1929–39* (University of California Press, 1986), p. 72.
3. B. E. Supple, *Commercial Crisis and Change in England, 1600–1642: A Study in the Instability of a Mercantile Economy*, (Cambridge University Press, 1959), p. 9.
4. These dates are based on the National Bureau of Economic Research list of U.S. business cycles. Business cycle dates may be different for other countries.
5. Paul Krugman, *The Return of Depression Economics* (W. W. Norton, 1999), p. 103.
6. Lawrence H. Summers, speech presented to the New York Economic Club, September 8, 1999.
7. Robert Sobel, *RCA* (Stein & Day, 1986), p, 35.
8. Barry Eichengreen and Peter Temin, "The Gold Standard and the Great Depression," National Bureau of Economic Research Working Paper No. 6060, June 1997, p. 38.

CHAPTER TWO

1. The term "New Economy" actually dates back to the early 1980s, when it had a very different meaning: an economy driven by services rather than

manufacturing. Thus, a well-known 1981 book was entitled *Services: The New Economy*, and the New Economy Fund, a mutual fund started in 1983, only invested in service-sector companies. The worry was that the service-driven New Economy was going to be marked by slow growth, rising prices, and the creation of armies of low-wage jobs. But starting in the early 1990s, the meaning of the term "New Economy" gradually morphed, as *Business Week* and others began using it to describe a technology-driven, fast-growing, low-inflation economy.

2. The break in the trend of productivity growth appears to have come in the third quarter of 1995; the break in the trend of GDP growth appears to have come in the first quarter of 1996; and the break in the trend of core inflation appears to have come in the second quarter of 1995.

3. Kathy Rebello, "Inside Microsoft," *Business Week*, July 15, 1996.

4. U.S. Bureau of the Census, *Historical Statistics of the United States* (U.S. Bureau of the Census, 1975), p. 734.

5. Peter Drucker, *Innovation and Entrepreneurship: Practice and Principles* (Harper & Row, 1985), pp. 127–28.

6. Paul Gompers and Josh Lerner, "Risk and Reward in Private Equity Investments: The Challenge of Performance Assessment," *Journal of Private Equity* (Winter 1997).

7. Samuel Kortum and Josh Lerner, "Does Venture Capital Spur Innovation?" National Bureau of Economic Research Working Paper No. 6846, December 1998.

8. Paul Gompers and Josh Lerner, *The Venture Capital Cycle* (MIT Press, 1999), p. 6.

9. Raghuram G. Rajan and Luigi Zingales, "Financial Systems, Industrial Structure, and Growth," paper prepared for the Symposium on the International Competitiveness of the Swedish Financial Industry, 1999.

10. Oliver Pfirrmann, Udo Wupperfeld, and Joshua Lerner, *Venture Capital and New Technology Based Firms: A US-German Comparison* (Physica-Verlag, 1997), p. 27.

11. Ibid., p. 31.

12. Mike Wright and Ken Robbie, editors, *Venture Capital* (Dartmouth, 1997), p. 75.

13. In addition, other countries may simply not have deep enough capital markets to absorb the almost inevitable large losses. For example, in the 1980s, U.S. venture capitalists lost about $500 million on failed mini-supercomputer makers (*New York Times*, October 8, 1989). They also took large losses on startups that were intended to exploit superconductor technology, which to date has not panned out commercially.

14. Clayton Christensen, *The Innovator's Dilemma* (Harvard Business School Press, 1997), pp. 155–56.

15. Pfirrmann et al., *Venture Capital and New Technology Based Firms*, p. 42.

16. Cynthia Robbins-Roth, *From Alchemy to IPO: The Business of Biotechnology* (Perseus, 2000), p. 175.

17. Steven Syre and Charles Stein, "Boston Capital," *Boston Globe*, February 18, 2000.

18. See, for example, Gompers and Lerner, *The Venture Capital Cycle*, p. 289; Wright and Robbie, *Venture Capital*, p. 399; and Thomas Mellmann and Manju Puri, "The Interaction Between Product Market and Financing Strategy: The Role of Venture Capital," Stanford Graduate School of Business Research Paper No. 1561, May 1999.

19. See, for example, Steven Kaplan and Per Stromberg, "Financial Contracting Theory Meets the Real World: An Empirical Analysis of Venture Capital Contracts," National Bureau of Economic Research Working Paper No. 7660, and Ronald Gilson and Bernard Black, "Does Venture Capital Require an Active Stock Market?" *Journal of Applied Corporate Finance* (Winter 1999).

20. According to the Bureau of Labor Statistics, productivity in the grocery industry fell by almost 10% from 1987 to 1998.

21. Catherine Mann, *Is the U.S. Trade Deficit Sustainable?* (Institute for International Economics, 1999), p. 58.

22. William Sahlman, "The New Economy Is Stronger Than You Think," *Harvard Business Review* (November–December 1999), p. 99.

23. The history of the private competitor is complicated. In 1992 the nonprofit Institute for Genetic Research was established by Craig Venter to map the human genome, funded by a ten-year, $70 million grant from HealthCare Investment Corporation, a venture capital firm. The condition of the grant was that Human Genome Sciences, a for-profit company also backed by the venture firm, had marketing rights to any commercial discoveries. In May 1997 this relationship was dissolved, and a year later a new for-profit company, Celera Genomics, was created by Venter to generate and commercialize "genomic information."

CHAPTER THREE

1. T. H. Watkins, *The Great Depression: America in the 1930s* (Little, Brown, 1993), p. 55.

2. William S. Rukeyser, "Pardon Me, But Is This Armageddon?" *Fortune*, February 6, 1995.

3. Sean Dennis Cashman, *America in the Twenties and Thirties* (New York University Press, 1989), p. 115.

4. Lendol Calder, *Financing the American Dream: A Cultural History of Consumer Credit* (Princeton University Press, 1999), pp. 184–85.

5. Ibid., p. 201.

6. Peter Temin, *Did Monetary Forces Cause the Great Depression?* (W. W. Norton, 1976), p. 131. See also *Historical Statistics of the United States,* p. 989.

7. Wesley Clair Mitchell, *Business Cycles* (University of California–Berkeley, 1913), p. 584.

8. Temin, "The Causes of American Business Cycles," p. 49.

9. William Barber, *From New Era to New Deal* (Cambridge University Press, 1985), p. 4.

10. Bertram Austin and W. Francis Lloyd, *The Secret of High Wages* (Dodd, Mead, 1926), p. 5.

11. Ibid., p. 24.

12. Milton Friedman and Anna Schwartz, *A Monetary History of the United States: 1867–1960* (National Bureau of Economic Research, 1963), p. 240.

13. Ibid., p. 10.

14. Alvin Hansen, *Business Cycles and National Income* (W. W. Norton, 1951, 1964), p. 513.

15. Rexford Tugwell, *Industry's Coming of Age* (Harcourt, Brace, 1927), p. 95.

16. Hansen, *Business Cycles and National Income,* p. 395.

17. Brookings Institution, *The Recovery Problem in the United States* (Brookings Institution, 1936), p. 207.

18. For both New York and Texas, employment changes are measured from January 1930 to January 1931. *Handbook of Labor Statistics,* 1931, No. 541, pp. 156–57.

19. Cashman, *America in the Twenties and Thirties,* p. 121.

20. Barber, *From New Era to New Deal,* p. 107.

21. Watkins, *The Great Depression,* p. 52.

22. Robert McElvaine, *The Great Depression* (Times Books, 1984), p. 91.

23. Karen Pennar, "The '20s and the '80s: Can Deflation Turn into Depression?" *Business Week,* June 9, 1986.

CHAPTER FOUR

1. See William Safire, "On Language," *New York Times,* January 23, 1994.

2. Alan Murray, *The Wealth of Choices* (Crown, 2000), p. 61.

3. To be more precise, labor productivity is determined by three factors: the amount of capital per worker; the skill level and education of workers; and a residual term called "multifactor productivity," which is often interpreted as the effects of technology. Virtually all macroeconomic forecasting models assume that the last two factors grow at a constant rate over the course of the business cycle.

4. F. M. Scherer, *New Perspectives on Economic Growth and Technological Innovation* (Brookings Institution, 1999), p. 72.

5. To be more precise, there is a negative correlation between annual

changes in nominal disposable income and annual changes in the S&P 500 index (averaged over the year) for the 1950–99 period. Part of this reflects the distortionary effects of inflation in the 1970s—which boosted nominal incomes and killed the stock market—but it's true for the 1980s and 1990s as well.

6. See, for example, Paul A. Gompers and Josh Lerner, *The Venture Capital Cycle* (MIT Press, 1999).

7. Scherer, *New Perspectives on Economic Growth and Technological Innova tion*, p. 75.

8. T. A. Heppenheimer, "Investors Tighten Grip on Venture Capital," *The Scientist*, September 3, 1990

9. Michael Schrage, "Venture Capital Loses Spirit of Adventure," *Los Angeles Times*, September 5, 1991.

10. Jonathan Weber, "Dream of Striking It Rich Fading in Silicon Valley," *Los Angeles Times*, September 9, 1991.

11. Josh Lerner and Alexander Tsai, "Do Equity Financing Cycles Matter?" National Bureau of Economic Research Working Paper No. 7464, January 2000.

12. This is based on the firms that reported both R&D and capital spending as of mid-May 2000.

13. Kevin Kelly, *New Rules for the New Economy* (Viking, 1998), p. 25.

14. Mary Finn, "The Increasing-Returns-to-Scale/Sticky-Price Approach to Monetary Analysis," *Economic Quarterly* (Federal Reserve Bank of Richmond, September 1995).

CHAPTER FIVE

1. As measured by the quarterly price indices for business investment in information technology published by the Bureau of Economic Analysis, which attempts to adjust for quality and technological improvements. These indices are better at capturing improvements in computing power— a faster microprocessor, for example—than improvements in either software or communications capabilities.

2. The information technology components of GDP include business spending on information technology equipment and software, consumer spending on computers and telecom services, and government spending on computers. All these figures are adjusted for imports and exports as well.

3. Alan Greenspan, Humphrey–Hawkins testimony to Congress, February 17, 2000.

4. See Michael Mandel, "The Prosperity Gap," *Business Week*, September 27, 1999.

5. See Standard & Poor's, *Security Price Index Record*, 1998.

6. Frederick Lewis Allen, *Only Yesterday*, (Harper, 1931) p. 310.

7. Charles Kindleberger, *Manias, Panics, and Crashes* (Basic Books, 1978), p. 101.

8. Stephen G. Cecchetti, "Wealth and Consumption: Would a Stock Market Drop Really Cause a Recession?" Occasional Essays on Current Policy Issues No. 4, February 2000.

9. Sydney Ludvigson and Charles Steindel, "How Important Is the Stock Market Effect on Consumption?" *Economy Policy Review*, Federal Reserve Bank of New York, July 1999.

10. *Business Week*, December 25, 1929, p. 24.

11. Kindleberger, *The World in Depression*, p. 117.

12. Temin, *Did Monetary Forces Cause the Great Depression?* p. 82.

13. *Business Week*, July 9, 1930, p. 5.

14. *Business Week*, August 20, 1930, cover.

15. "Tighten Money, Japan," *The Economist*, May 26, 1990.

16. "Interest Rates: Have They Finally Peaked?" *Japan Economic Journal*, November 3, 1990.

17. "Monetary Policy Attacked," *Japan Economic Journal*, December 22, 1990.

CHAPTER SIX

1. There is no good official definition of depression. A recession is typically defined as two or more consecutive quarters of negative economic growth. The official arbiter of recessions, the Business Cycle Dating Committee at the National Bureau of Economic Research, defines a recession as "a recurring period of decline in total output, income, employment, and trade, usually lasting from six months to a year, and marked by widespread contractions in many sectors of the economy." By contrast, they define depression, rather vaguely, as a "recession that is major in both scale and duration."

2. Peter Temin, "The Causes of American Business Cycles," in Jeffrey Fuhrer and Scott Schuh, eds., *Beyond Shocks: What Causes Business Cycles?* Federal Reserve Bank of Boston Conference Series No. 42, June 1998, p. 43.

3. Ibid., p. 45.

4. Eichengreen and Temin, "The Gold Standard and the Great Depression," p. 19.

5. Kindleberger, *The World in Depression*, p. 119.

6. *Business Week*, July 5, 1930, p. 40.

7. *Business Week* October 22, 1930, p. 40.

8. Laurence H. Meyer, speech presented to the Stern Graduate School of Business, New York University, November 30, 1999.

9. Carl Shapiro and Hal Varian, *Information Rules* (Harvard Business School Press, 1999), p. 1.

10. Federal Aviation Administration, "Stall and Spin Awareness Train-

ing," Advisory Circular No. 61–67B, 1991. Whether an airplane stalls is determined not just by its speed, but by its attitude, its configuration, whether it is turning, and a whole host of other factors. Similarly, it may also be hard to judge what the stall speed of the New Economy is.

11. Alan Greenspan, "Structural Change in the New Economy," speech presented to the National Governors' Association, July 11, 2000.

12. Paul Krugman, *Red Herring*, June 1998.

13. Robert Gordon, "Does the 'New Economy' Measure Up to the Great Inventions of the Past?" draft of paper written for the *Journal of Economic Perspectives*, May 2000.

14. Robert Samuelson, "Wall Street as Main Street," *Washington Post*, April 19, 2000.

15. Bob Davis, "Head Scratchers: To Campaigners 2000, Only Thing Missing in This Boom Is Why," *Wall Street Journal*, January 17, 2000.

16. John Garraty, *The Great Depression* (Harcourt Brace Jovanovich, 1986), p. 20.

17. Ibid., p. 34.

18. Ibid., p. 38.

19. The consensus forecast comes from the *Business Week* survey of forecasts in the December 22, 1973 issue. The actual figure for 1974 comes from the July 1975 version of the national income and product accounts. Both numbers refer to annual averages.

20. *Business Week*, December 21, 1974, p. 51.

21. The consensus forecast comes from the *Business Week* survey of forecasts in the December 28, 1981 issue. The actual figure for 1982 comes from the July 1983 revision of the national income and product accounts. Both numbers are measured from the fourth quarter of 1981 to the fourth quarter of 1982 (to correspond to the numbers reported by the survey).

22. W. Brian Arthur, *Increasing Returns and Path Dependence in the Economy* (University of Michigan Press), 1994, p. 1.

CHAPTER SEVEN

1. National Association of Colleges and Employers, Summer 2000 *Salary Survey*.

2. The exact number of new jobs depends on how much of that $50 billion in venture capital is immediately spent, and how much of it funds high-paying tech jobs versus spilling over to lower-paying positions in the overall economy.

3. Bureau of Labor Statistics, "Contingent and Alternative Employment Arrangements," February 1999.

4. Hewitt Associates U.S. Salary Increase Survey, released 1999.

5. Goldman Sachs, *The Pocket Chartroom*, February 2000.

CHAPTER EIGHT

1. John Eatwell and Lance Taylor, *Global Finance at Risk* (The New Press, 2000), p. 135.
2. Ibid., pp. 44–45.
3. Krugman, *The Return of Depression Economics*, p. 113.
4. Thomas Palley, "The Forces Making for an Economic Collapse: Why a Depression Could Happen," *Atlantic Monthly*, July 1996.
5. Willem Duisenberg, testimony before the Committee on Economic and Monetary Affairs of the European Parliament, June 20, 2000.
6. Kindleberger, *Mania, Panics and Crashes*, p. 223.
7. Eatwell and Taylor, *Global Finance at Risk*, p. 205.

CHAPTER NINE

1. *Business Week*, October 29, 1930, p. 40.
2. *Los Angeles Times* poll, May 9, 2000.
3. Rajan and Zingales, "The Great Reversals: The Politics of Financial Development in the 20th Century," working paper, June 2000.
4. Krugman, *The Return of Depression Economics*, p. 157.
5. Krugman, *The Return of Depression Economics*, p. 102.
6. Barry Bluestone and Bennett Harrison, *Growing Prosperity* (Houghton Mifflin, 2000), p. 20.
7. Ibid.
8. Paul Romer, "Should the Government Subsidize Supply or Demand in the Market for Scientists and Engineers?" National Bureau of Economic Research Paper No. 7723, June 2000.
9. Rajan and Zingales, "The Great Reversals: The Politics of Financial Development in the 20th Century."
10. Stephen Roach, "Architectural Reform: Managing Financial Market Volatility in the New Millennium," speech presented in South Korea, March 31, 2000.
11. E. Gerald Corrigan, "Resolving Financial Crises," speech presented in London, May 10, 2000.

CHAPTER TEN

1. One of the great economic failures of the second half of the twentieth century was the inability of nuclear power to live up to its hype as a cheap, safe form of energy. If it had come anywhere close to meeting its promises, the oil shock of the 1970s would have been far less harmful.
2. Richard McKenzie, *The Paradox of Progress* (Oxford University Press, 1997), p. 7.

Index